AF598919

ANDREAS VON BUDDENBROCK

THE INK TRAIL
HONG KONG

The Ink Trail: Hong Kong
ISBN 978-988-76748-6-3

Published by Blacksmith Books
Unit 26, 19/F, Block B, Wah Lok Industrial Centre,
37-41 Shan Mei Street, Fo Tan, Hong Kong
Tel: (+852) 2877 7899
www.blacksmithbooks.com

CONTENTS

THIS BOOK...

Toward the tail-end of 2017, I had an idea: to create a travel blog. A sketch-travel blog, to be more precise. I had been thinking of different ways in which I'd be able to "work" while doing the two things I like the most — drawing and traveling. I already had some sketches and pretty soon, after going over a number of names, I had decided that the blog was going to be called "The Ink Trail". If you didn't already catch it (and I wouldn't fault you if you didn't), the name was a play on words, relating to the famous Inca Trail in Peru, but also to the trail of ink - and ink drawings - left by my pen.

Soon enough, I had bought the domain name and a website was in the works. After a few weeks of figuring out Wordpress I finally had a page that was ready to be seen by the world! But who would even know of its existence? I needed a social media page for promotion. As luck would have it, "theinktrail" wasn't already taken as a username on Instagram and before long, my page was up and running.

Fast-forward about a year and it became clear to me that the website wasn't getting the traction I had hoped for (despite me being pretty consistent with my writing). But, the Instagram was doing better than ever. I had been diligent about sharing new sketches, starting on a new one each and every single week. By the end of 2018, I had a full Moleskine book worth of drawings, and by the end of 2019, another book was filled from start to finish. And so it kept going.

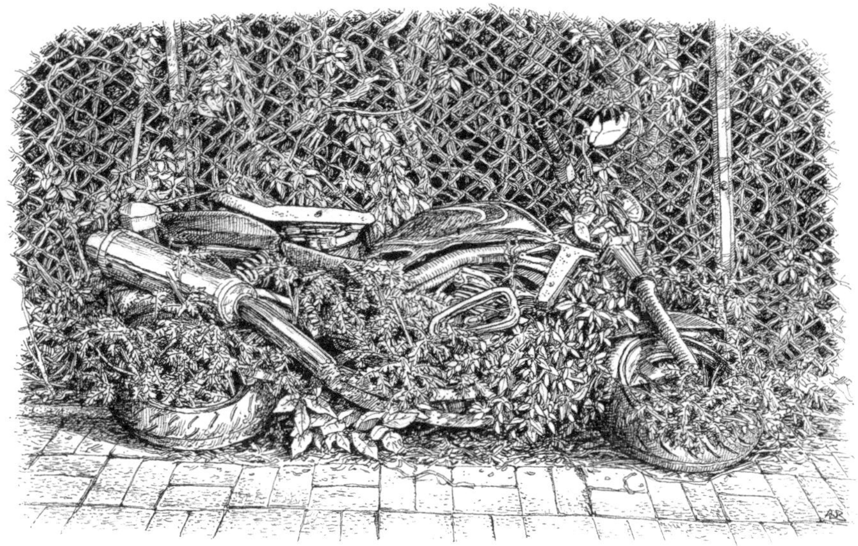

"Time Devours All Things" (2021), Lohas Park, Hong Kong

With a full-time art teaching job, the traveling I had envisioned wasn't happening nearly as often as I would have wished, but when it did, the sketchbook was always with me. Despite all this, however, most of my time was spent in Hong Kong (where I work and live), and thus my sketches from various locations around the city were piling up.

Which brings us to this very book. For a while, I had been thinking of getting a proper book together with my drawings from in and around Hong Kong, and well, here it is. You're holding it. Sure, there have been zines in previous years, and I've been proud of those as well, but they only contained a small selection of drawings from each respective year. This time, I've taken a larger number of my favorite drawings and put them all together in a book that, should my hopes and intentions come true, will inspire you to grab your pen, put on your hiking shoes and get out there on the trail.

I hope I'll see you there!

Andreas von Buddenbrock / "The Ink Trail"
October 2023

CHAPTER I

CONCRETE JUNGLE

I've been lucky to call Hong Kong my home for quite some time now. But what is it that makes this town so special, and why does it stand out so much from other cities around the world?

Ever since the day I first set foot here back in 2011 (stepping off the airport bus in Tsim Sha Tsui), I've been awed by the scale of the buildings, the juxtaposition between concrete and nature, the colorful signs and the oftentimes cluttered - yet all the more interesting - shops and establishments. Much like an organism, the heart of Hong Kong can be felt in every moment and in every nook and cranny of its buzzing streets, lit up from above by giant screens and neon lights.

All of this, I believe, comes together in a symphony of impressions that is unique to this city and makes it "stand out from the crowd".

That being said, however, I personally find architectural drawing (perspective, straight lines and symmetry) to be one of my least favorite aspects when re-creating urban environments. Take the drawing on the right-hand-side, for example, which portrays the famous "Monster Building" complex in Quarry Bay. It was something that I had long been wanting to draw — much because of its similarities with the old Kowloon City — but spending all that time using a ruler to make sure the perspective is on-point is, to be honest with you, not something I find particularly enjoyable (once ›ast it, however, everything becomes a lot more fun).

Right: "***Monster***" (2019)
Quarry Bay, Hong Kong

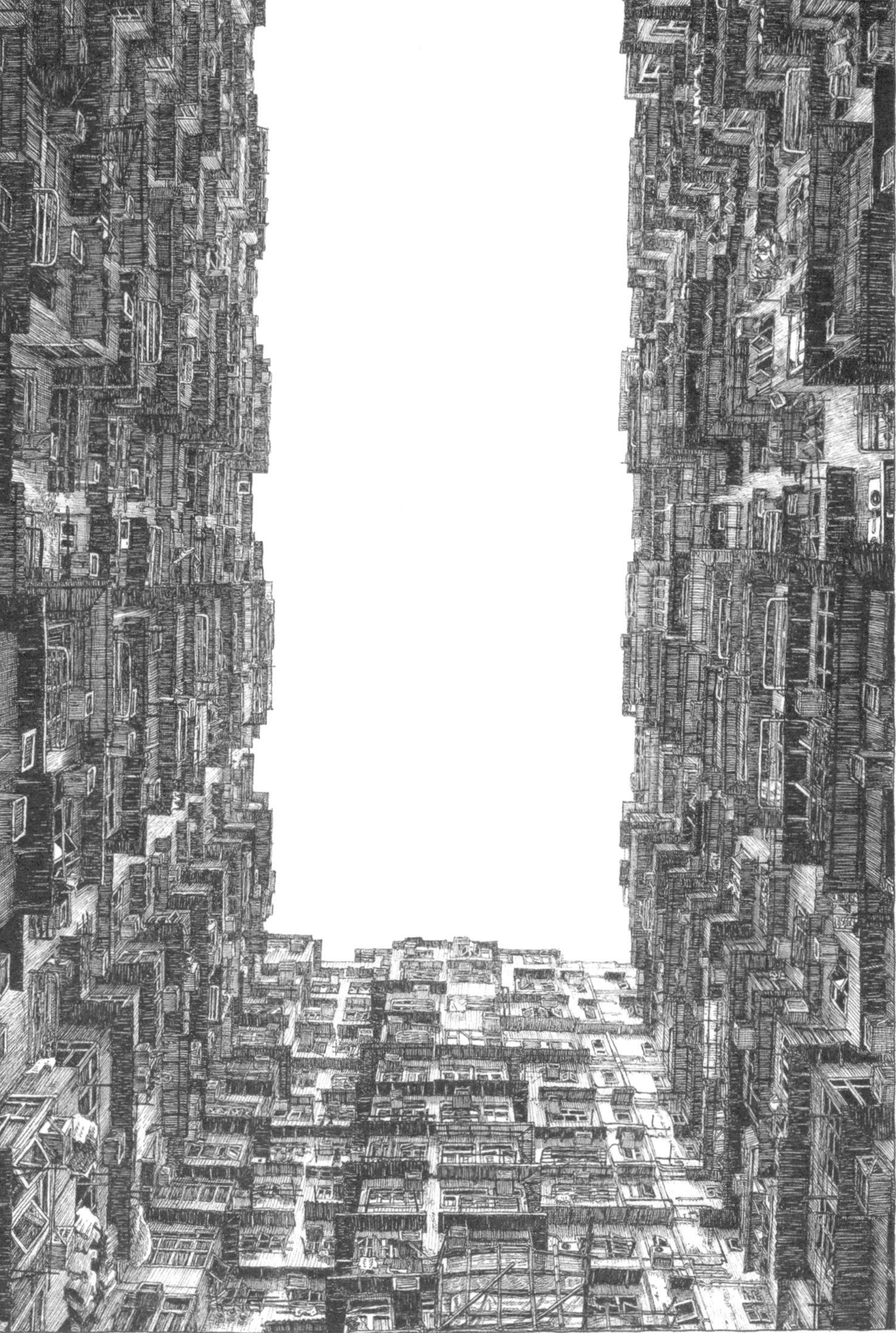

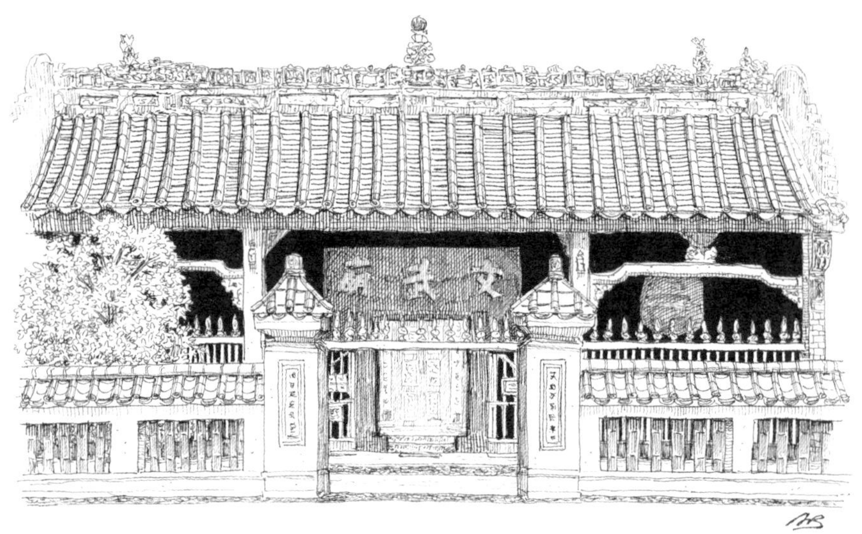

"Man Mo Temple" (2020)
Sheung Wan, Hong Kong

This is why, when drawing urban scenery, I tend to stay away from angular views of architecture and rather focus on the city way-up-close or from a greater distance. The latter is also due to my proclivity to hike and climb onto high vantage points in order to find (and draw) some of the most amazing views this city has to offer.

Finally, a city isn't anything without its citizens. Which is why I've decided to also include a small selection of drawings portraying Hong Kongers in the midst of their daily lives.

Right: ***"ICC"*** (2018)
Kowloon, Hong Kong

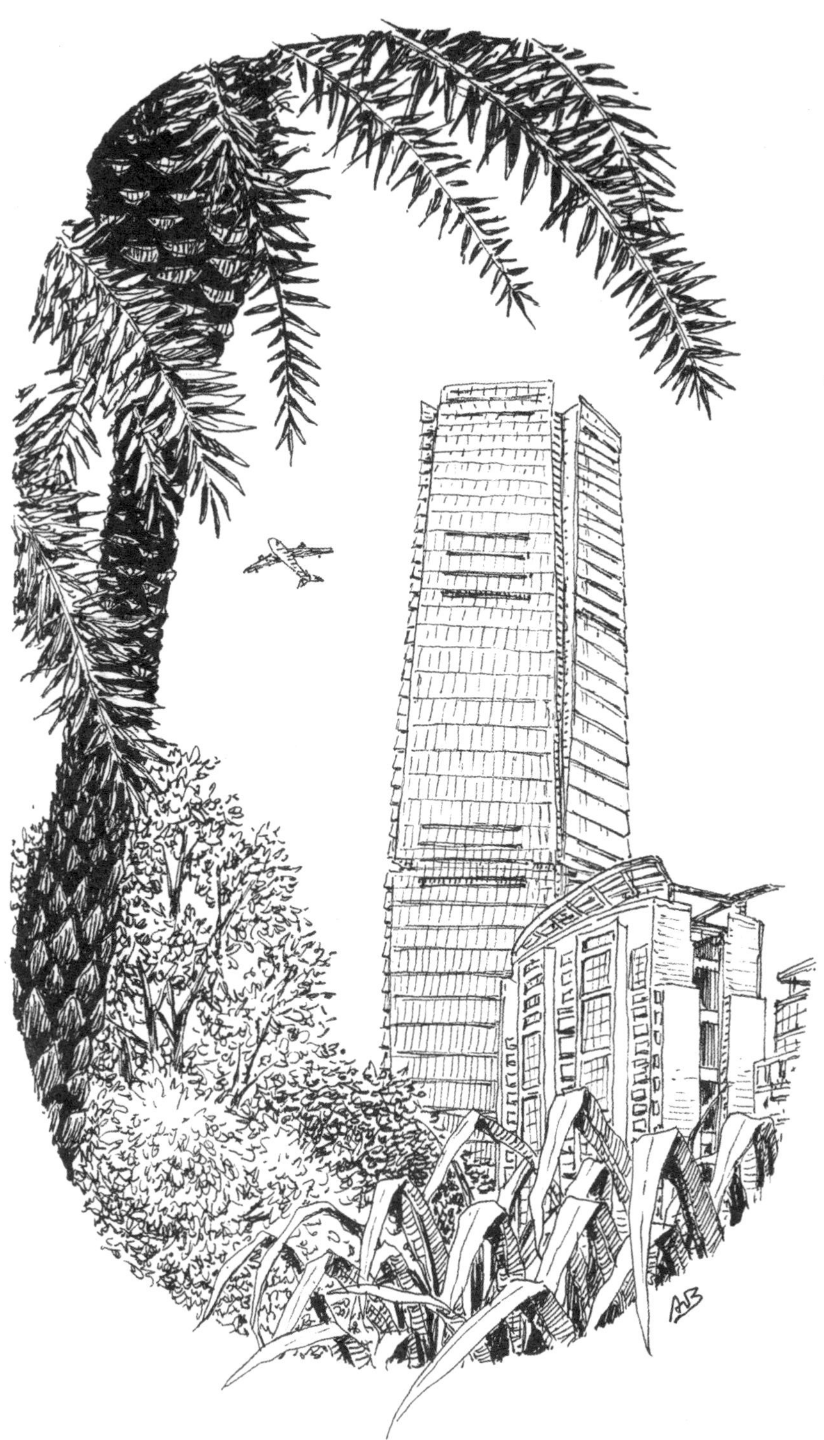

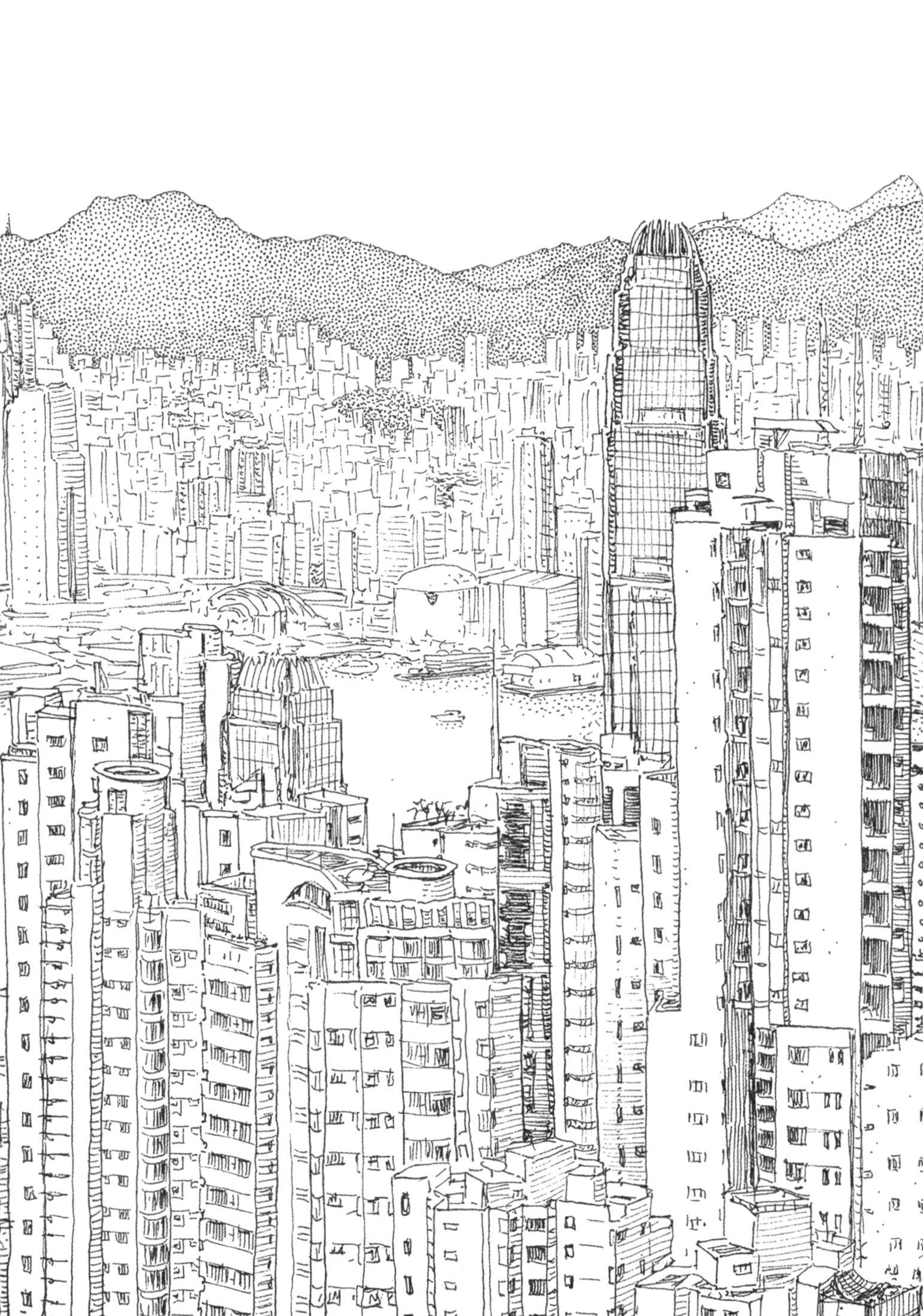

"Victoria Peak" (2018)
Victoria Peak, Hong Kong

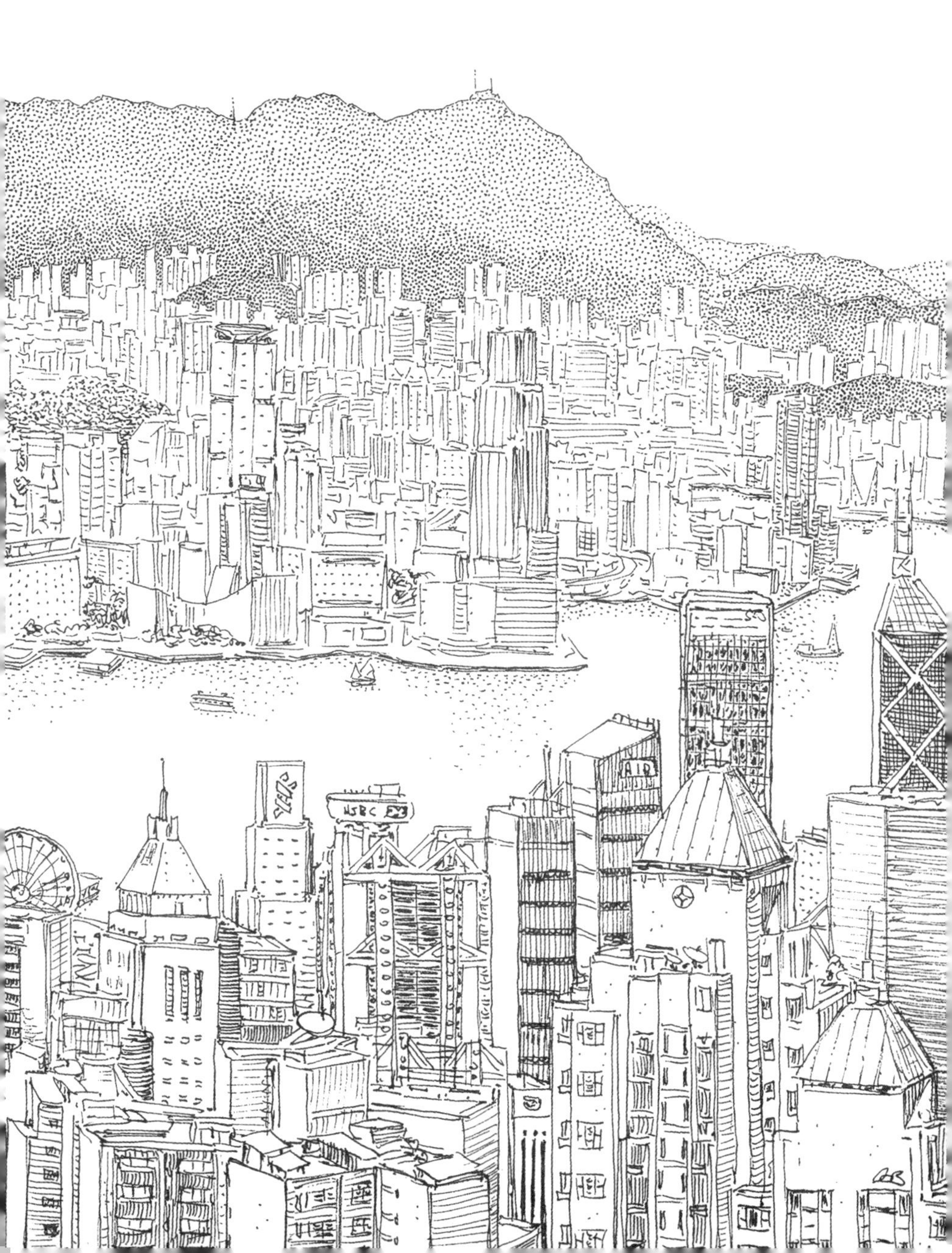

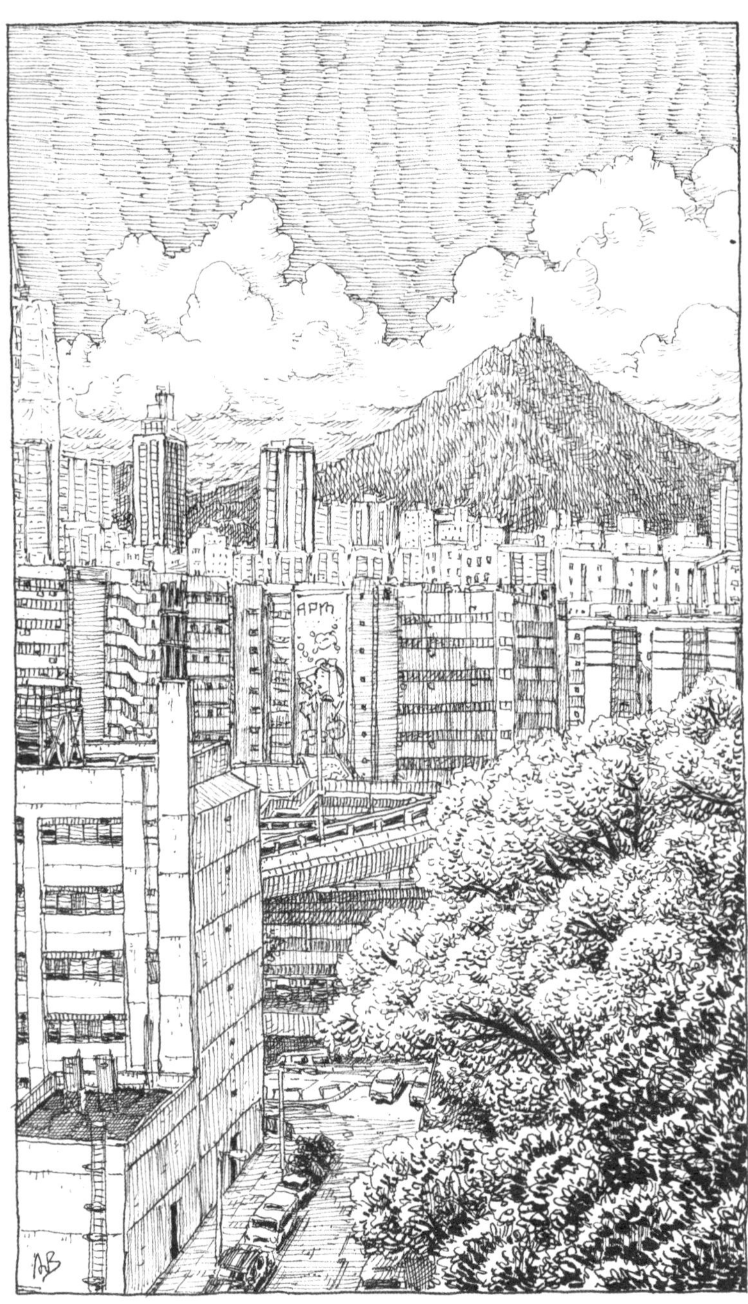

"Lam Tin" (2020)
Lam Tin, Hong Kong

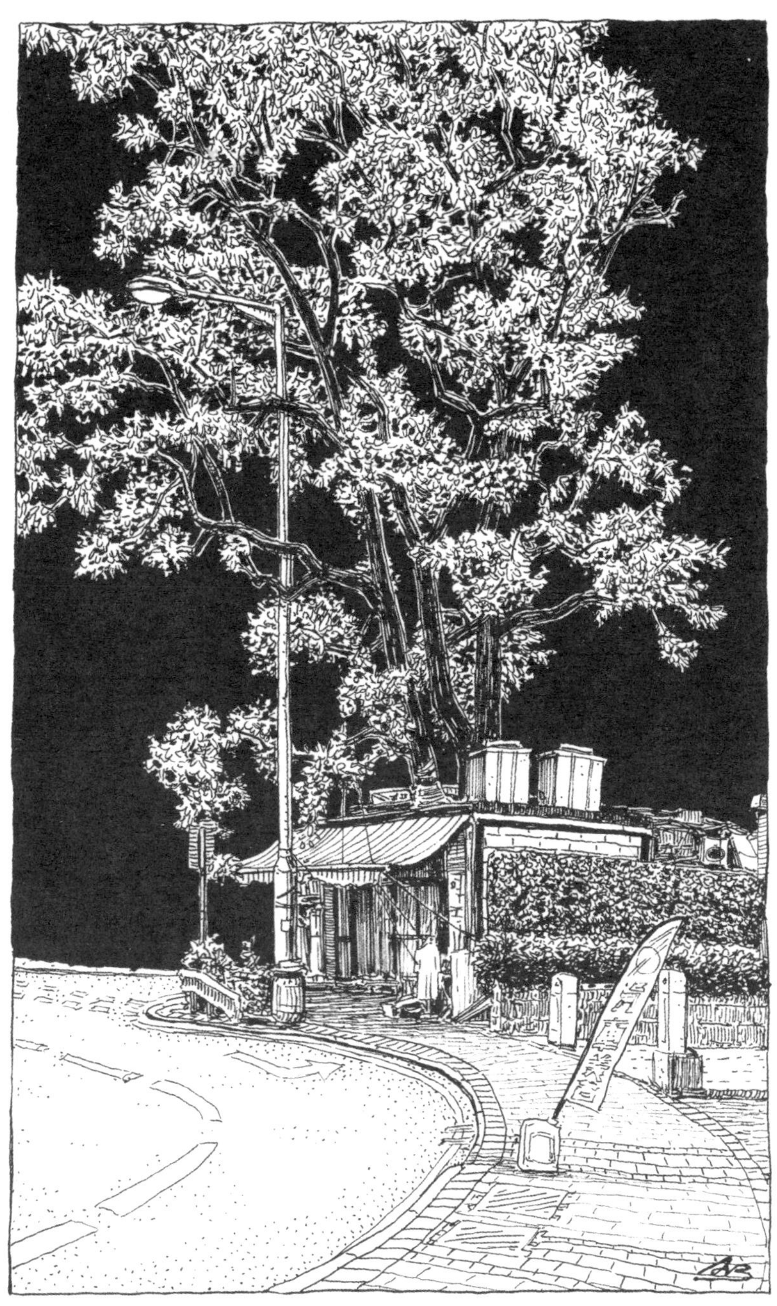

"Wong Chuk Hang" (2019)
Wong Chuk Hang, Hong Kong

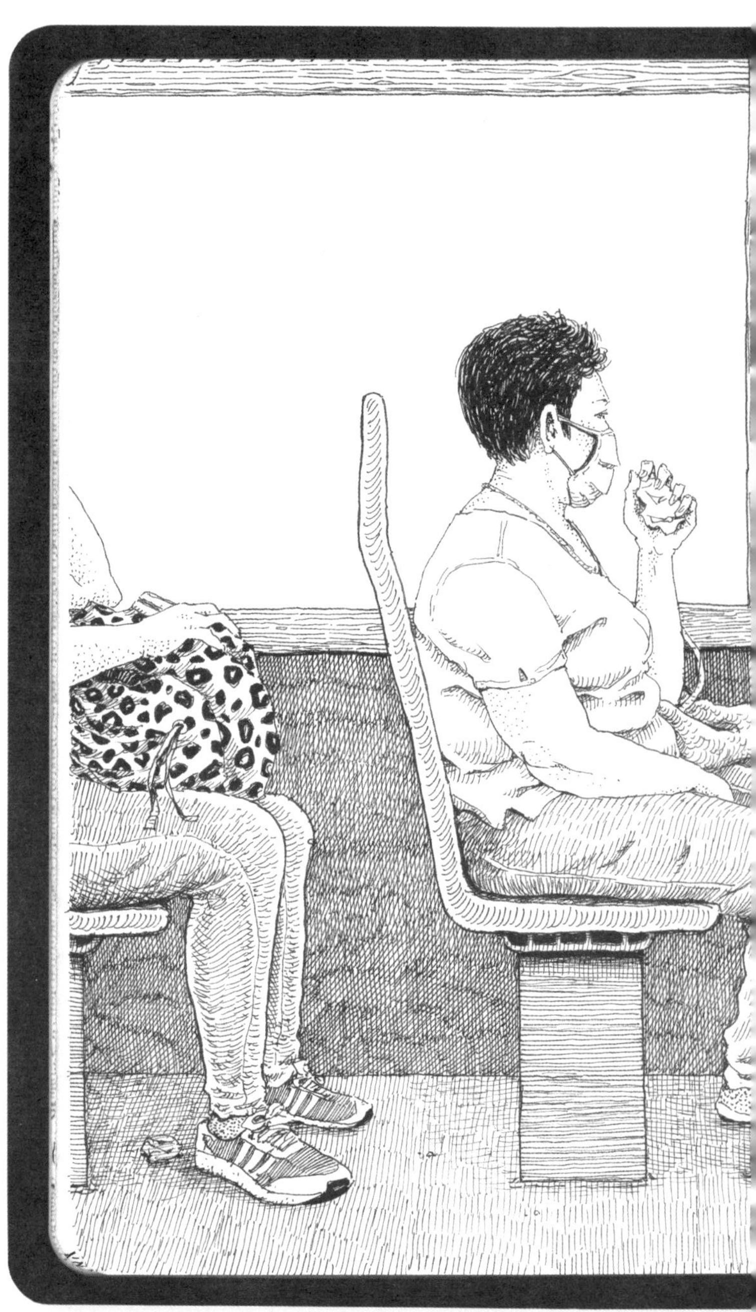

"Trams" (2020)
Hong Kong Island, Hong Kong

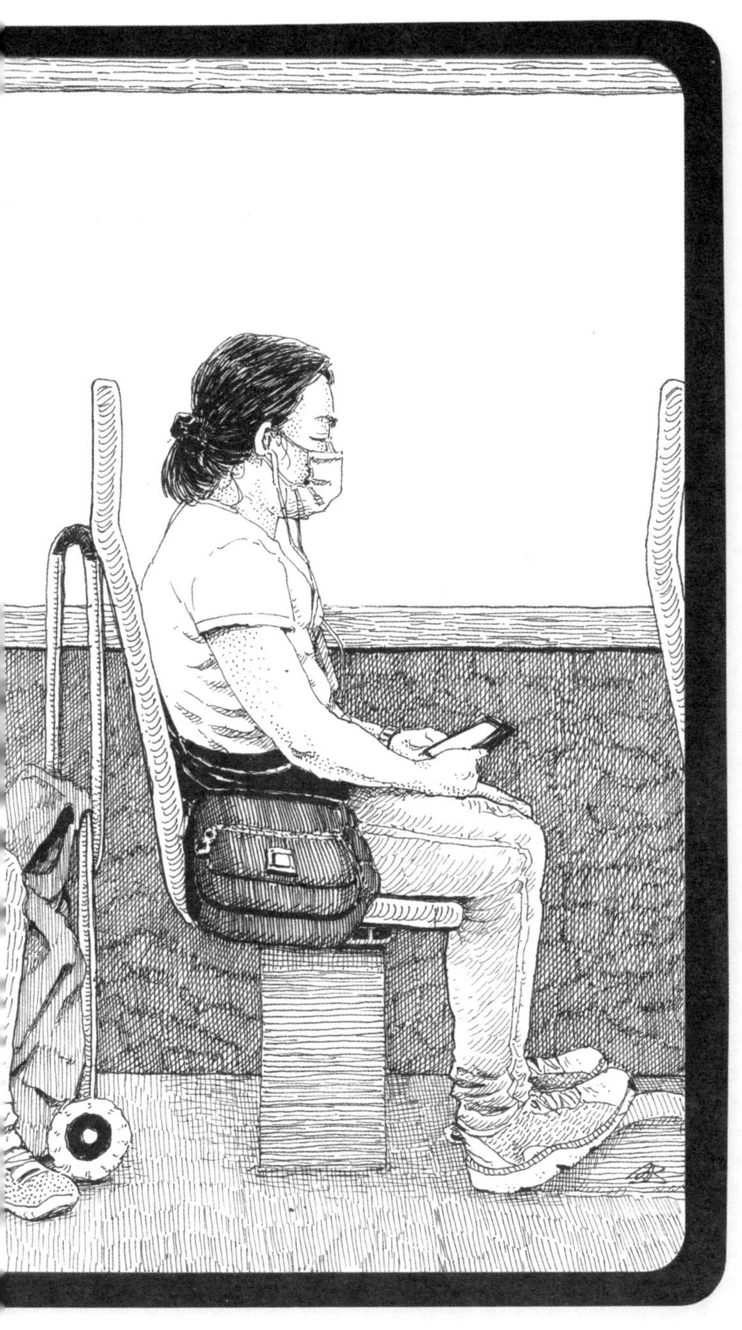

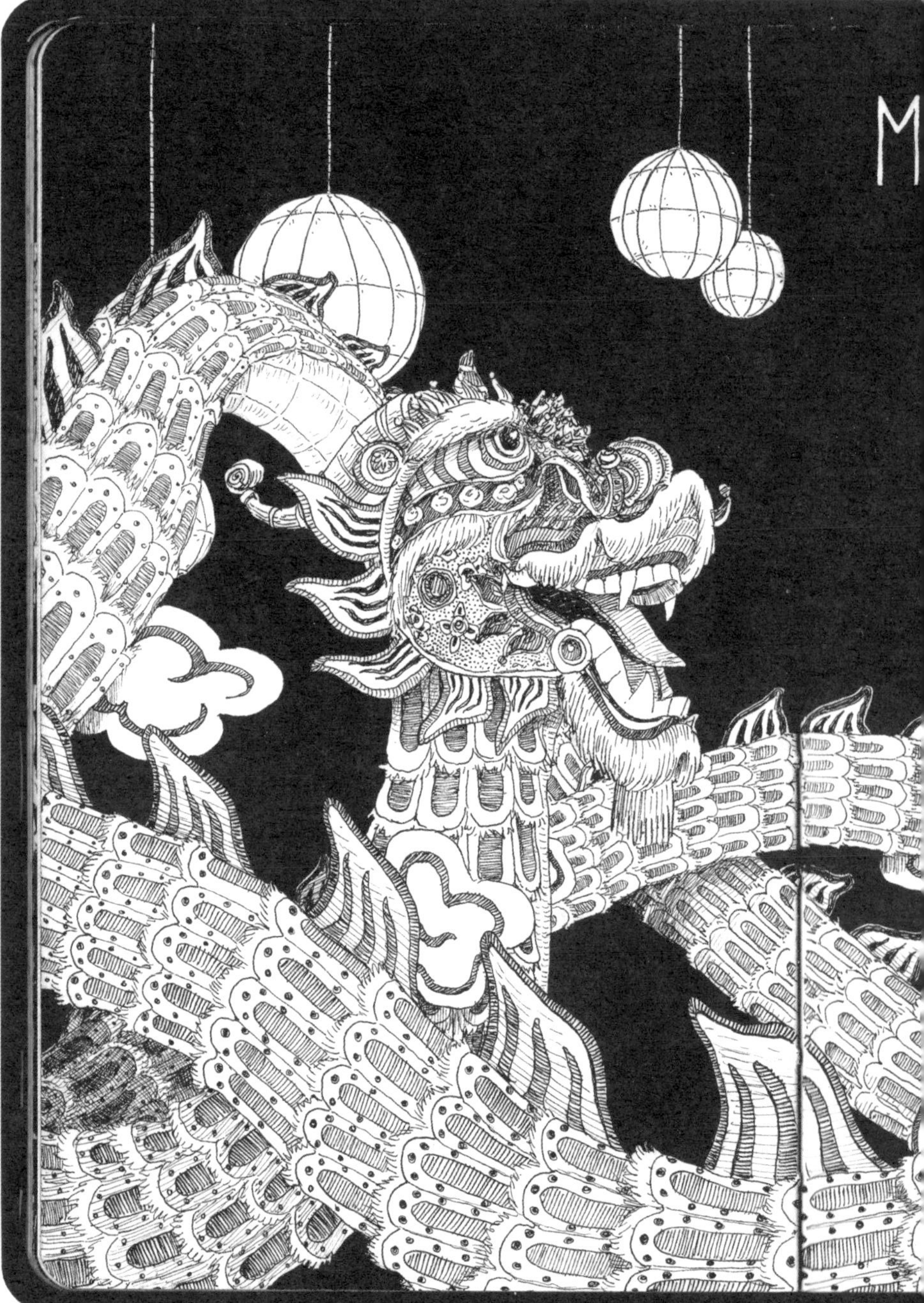

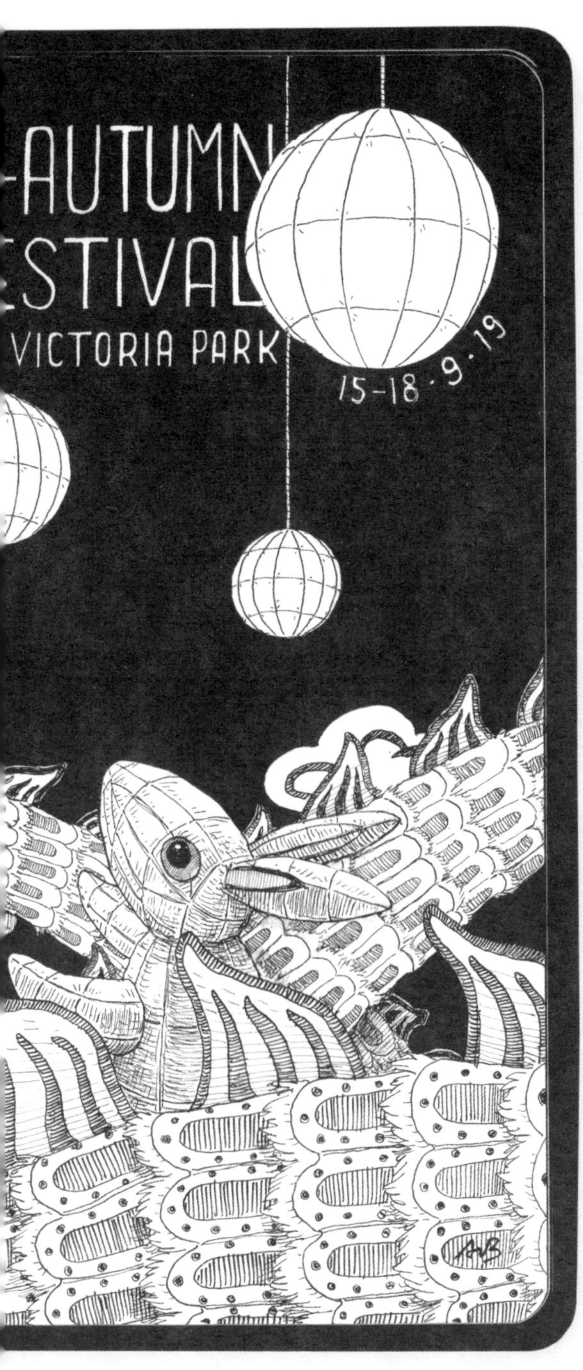

"Mid-Autumn Festival" (2019)
Causeway Bay, Hong Kong

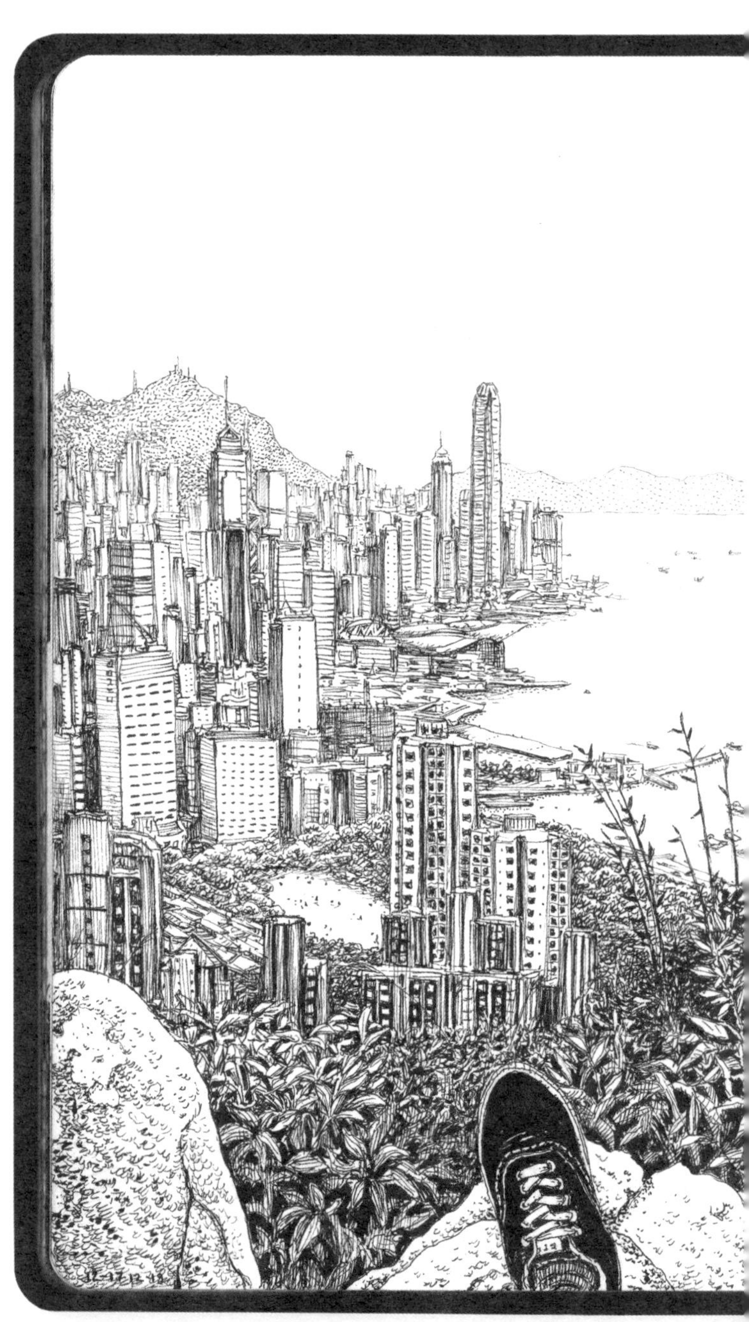

"New Horizons" (2019)
Braemar Hill, Hong Kong

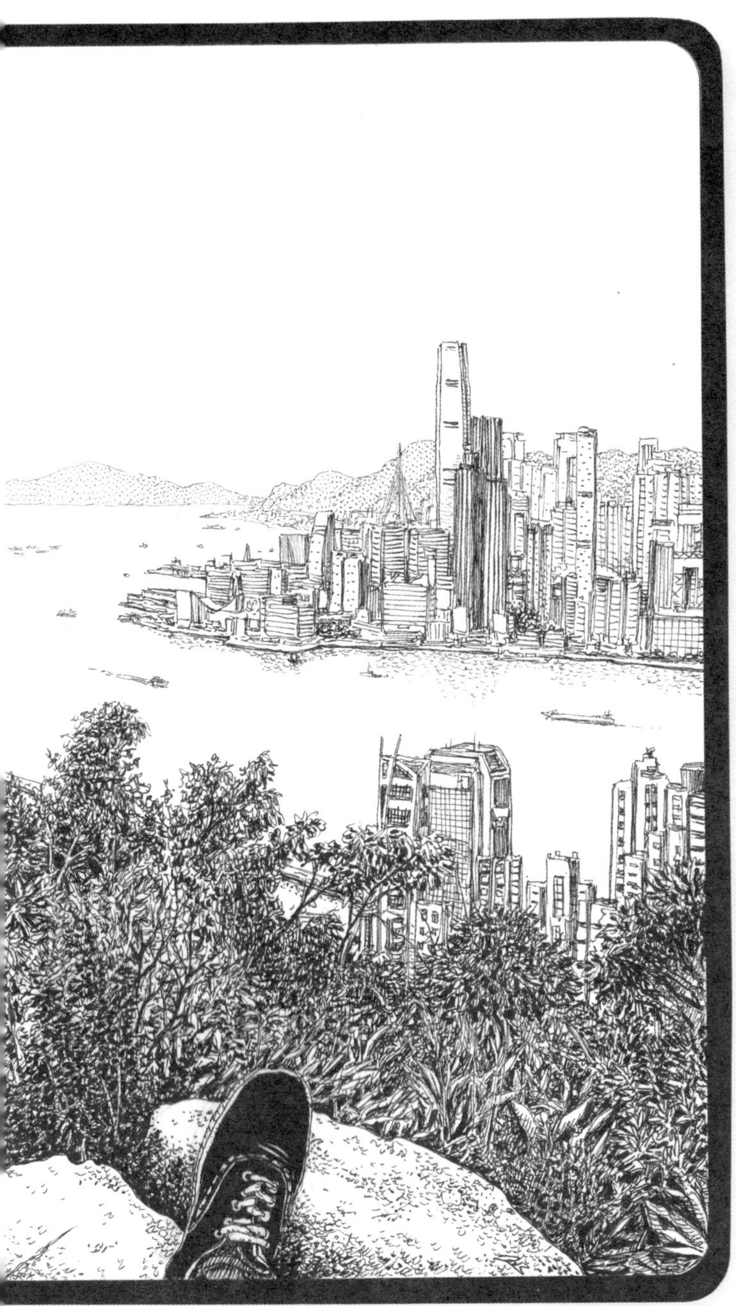

The area surrounding Yau Tong has been frequently visited by Yours Truly over the past few years. Aside from there being plenty of lunch, dinner and coffee places, there are plenty of other things to see and do if you just venture outside of the shopping malls.

I've spent a lot of time walking up the hiking path by Devil's Peak, either to visit the old Gough Battery ruins on top of the mountain or keep hiking along the Wilson Trail towards Tseung Kwan O. There's also the famous fish market down

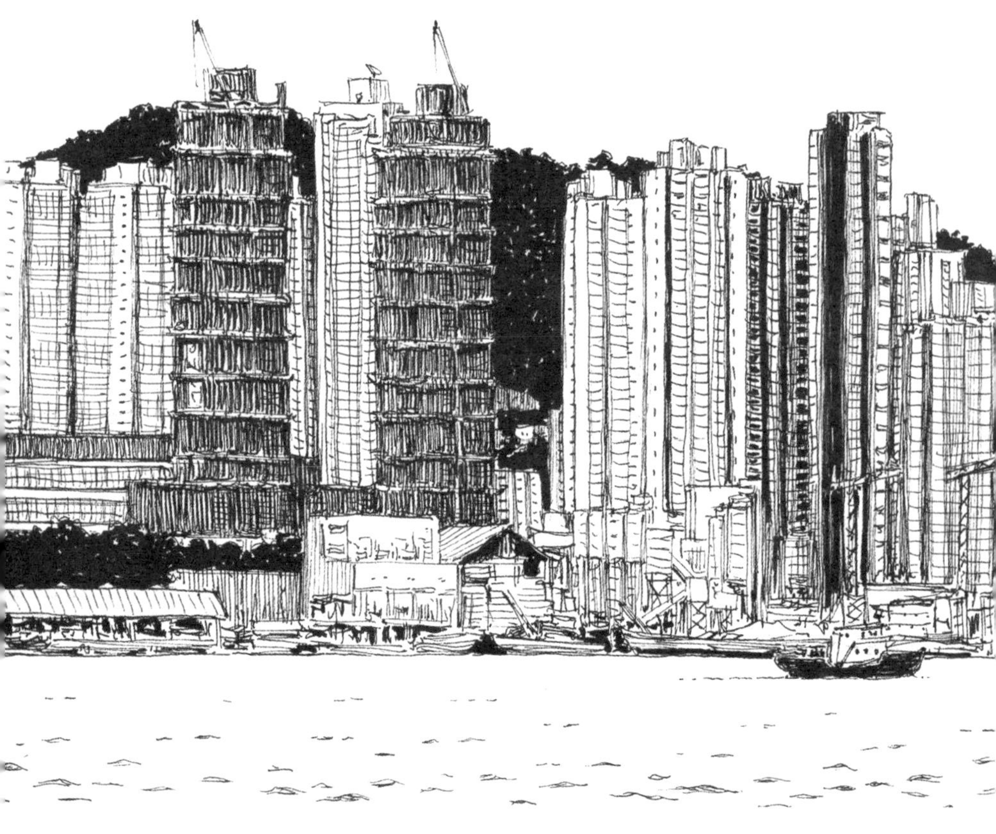

by the water (its bright neon signs can be seen from Hong Kong Island) and an old, abandoned stone quarry - but more about that in a following chapter.

Sometimes I just feel like having a more "urban walk". Then I might go for a stroll from the Yau Tong MTR station over to the old industrial buildings and boardwalks of Kwun Tong.

"Yau Tong" (2019)
Yau Tong, Hong Kong

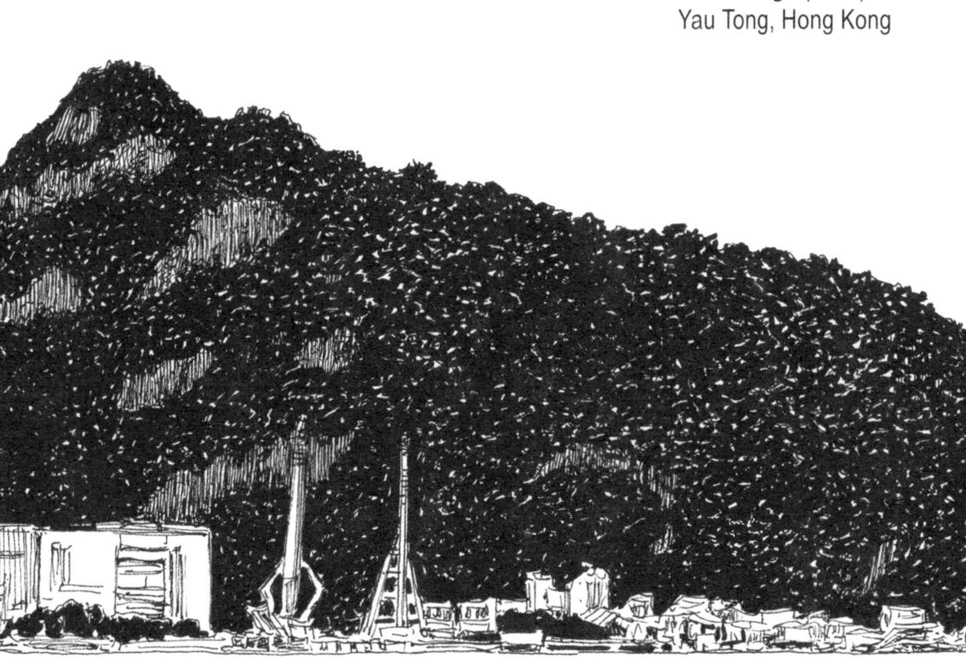

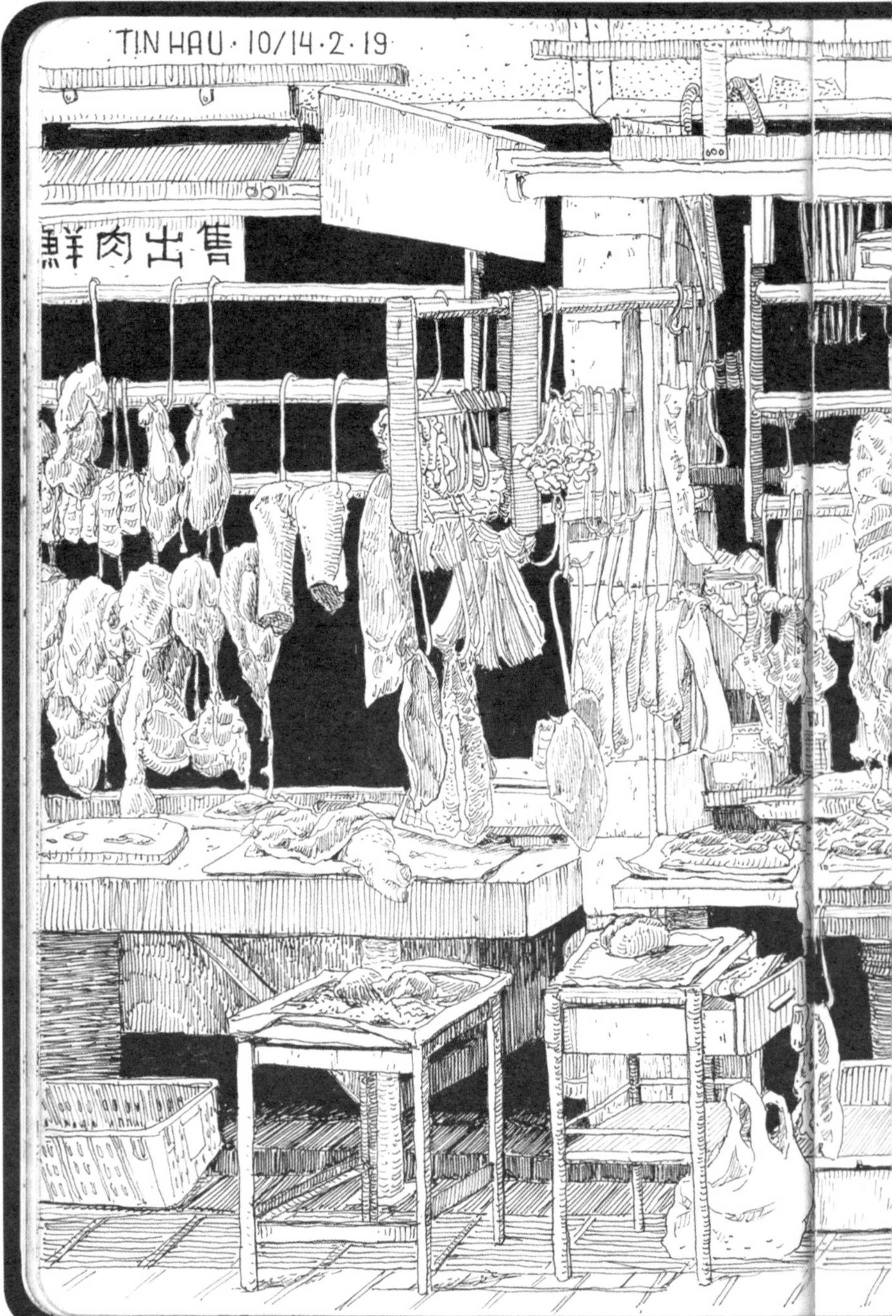
TIN HAU · 10/14·2·19
鮮肉出售

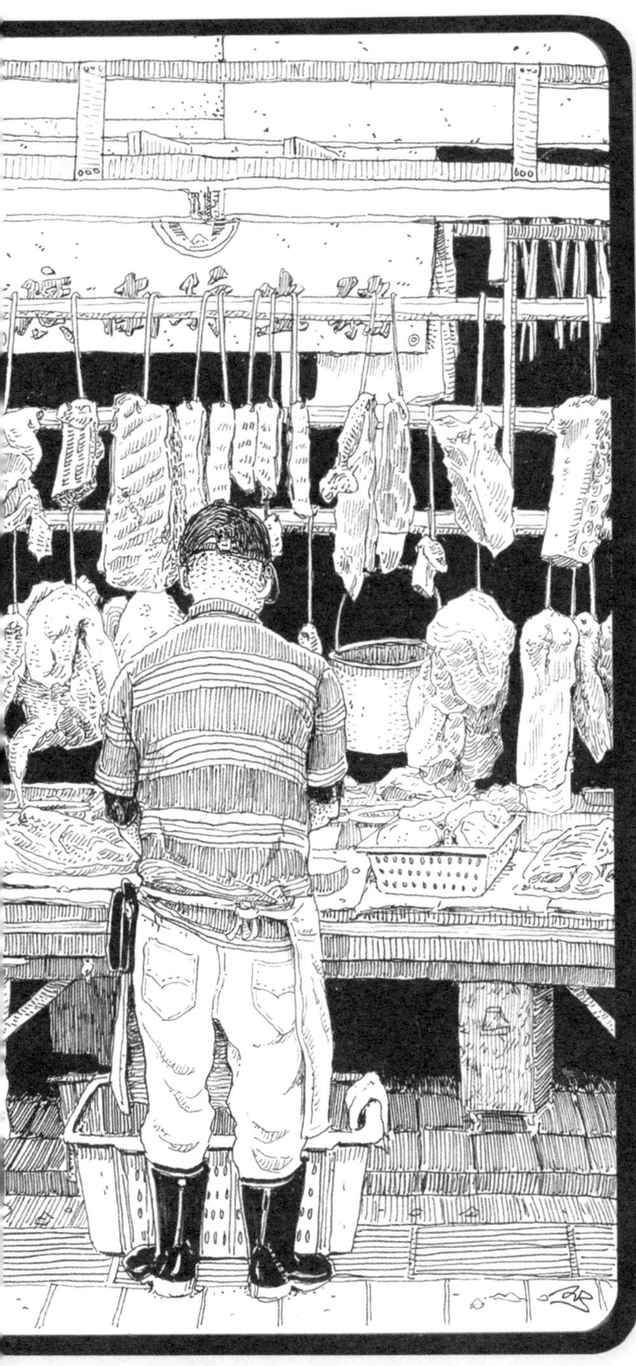

"Meat Market" (2019)
Tin Hau, Hong Kong

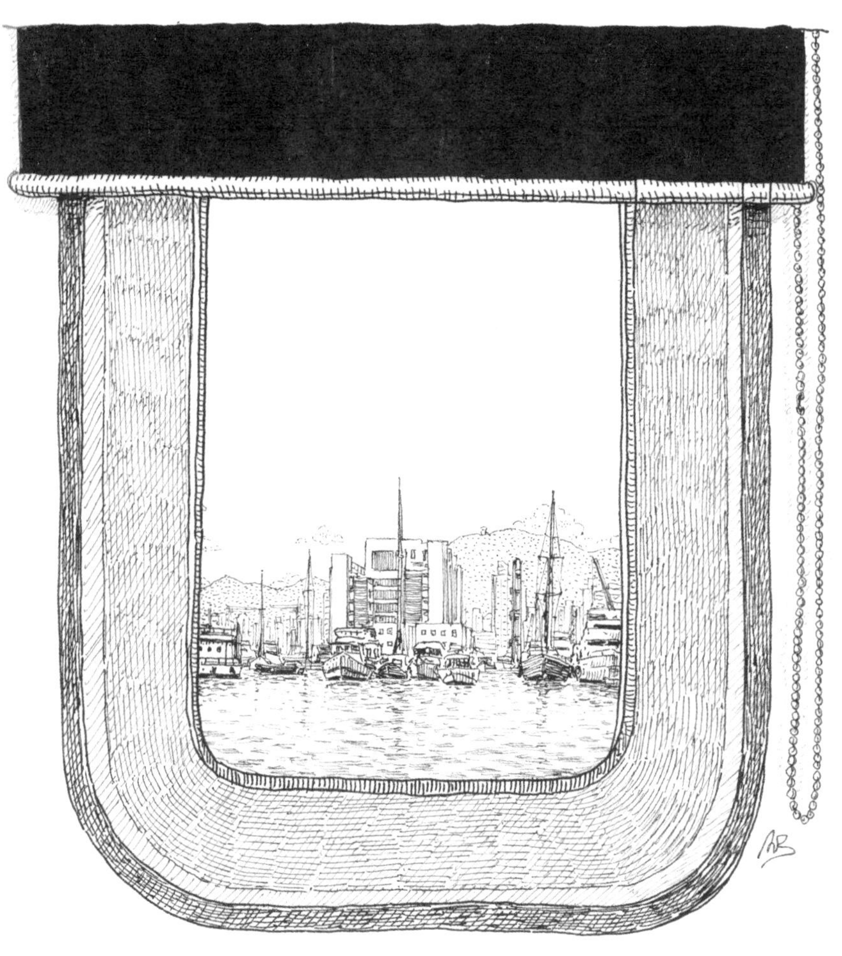

"Kwun Tong Harbour" (2020)
Kwun Tong, Hong Kong

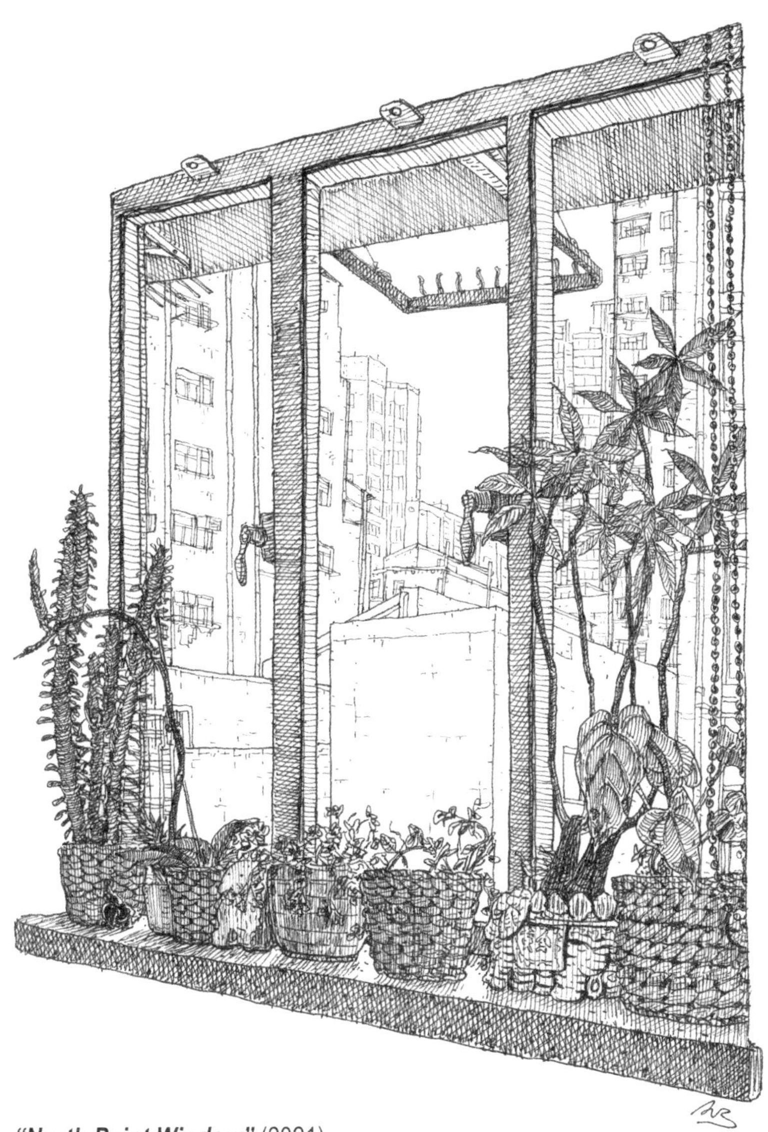

"North Point Window" (2021)
North Point, Hong Kong

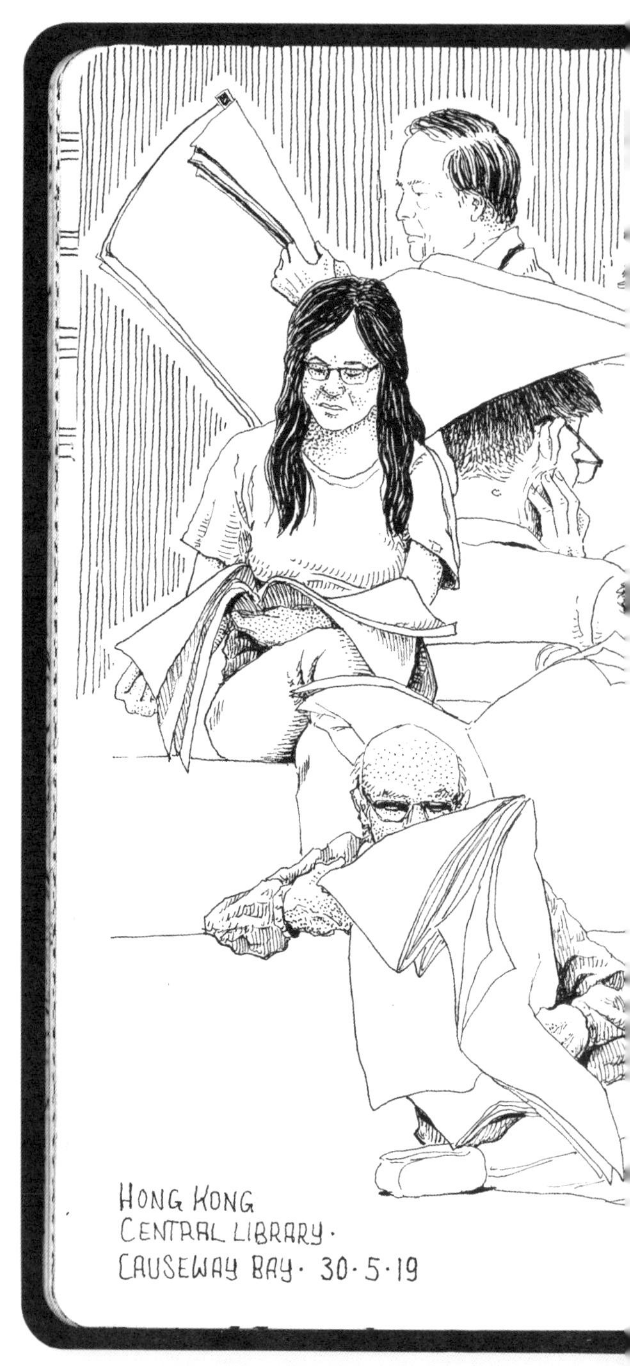

"HK Central Library" (2019)
Causeway Bay, Hong Kong

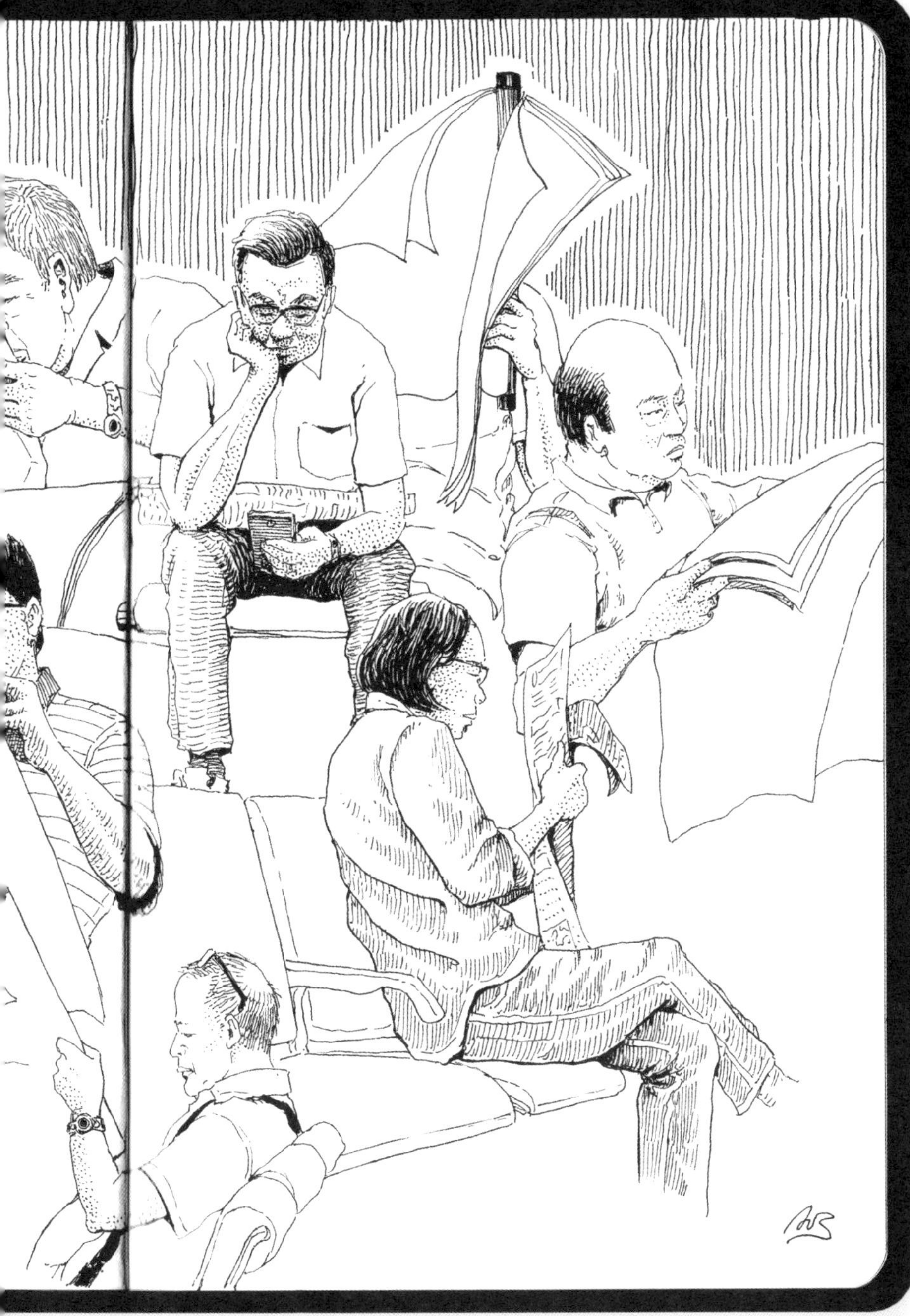

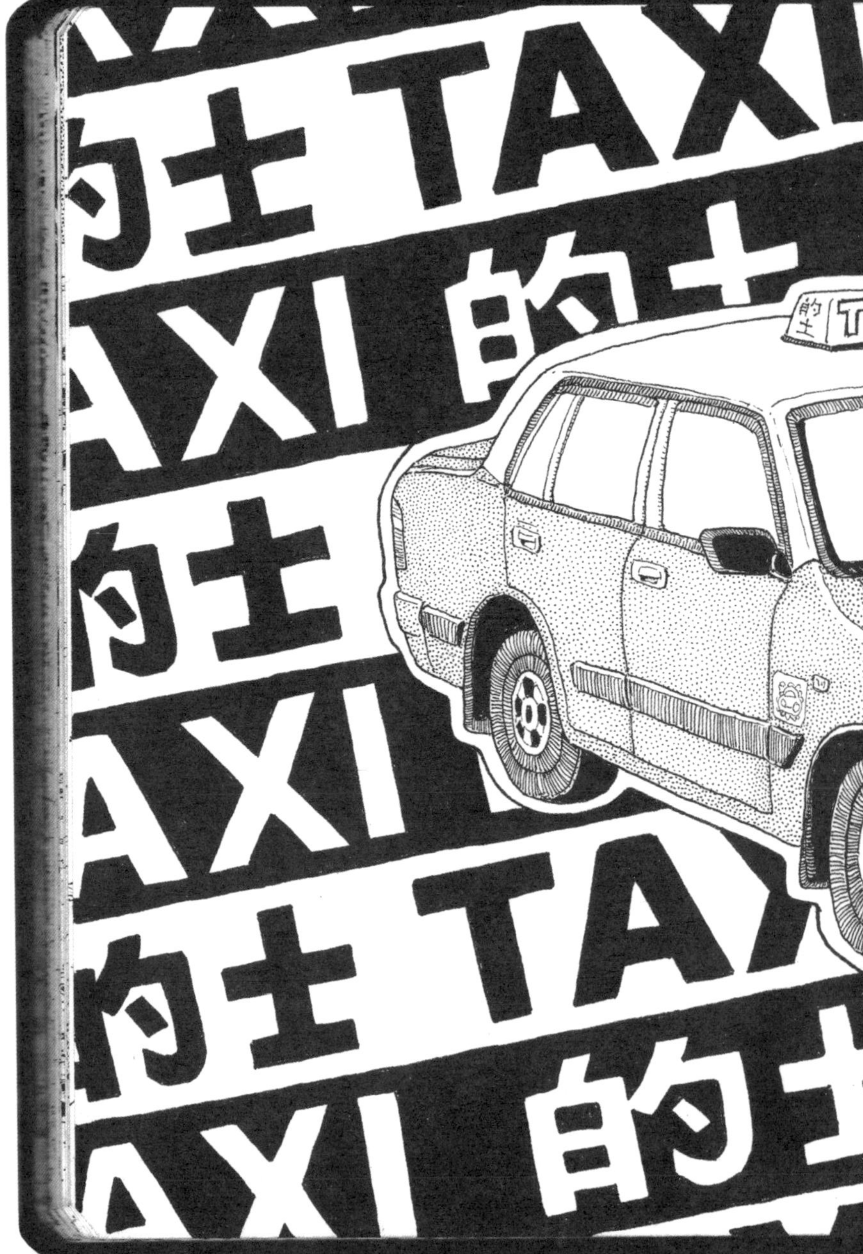
的士 TAXI
的士
的士
的士

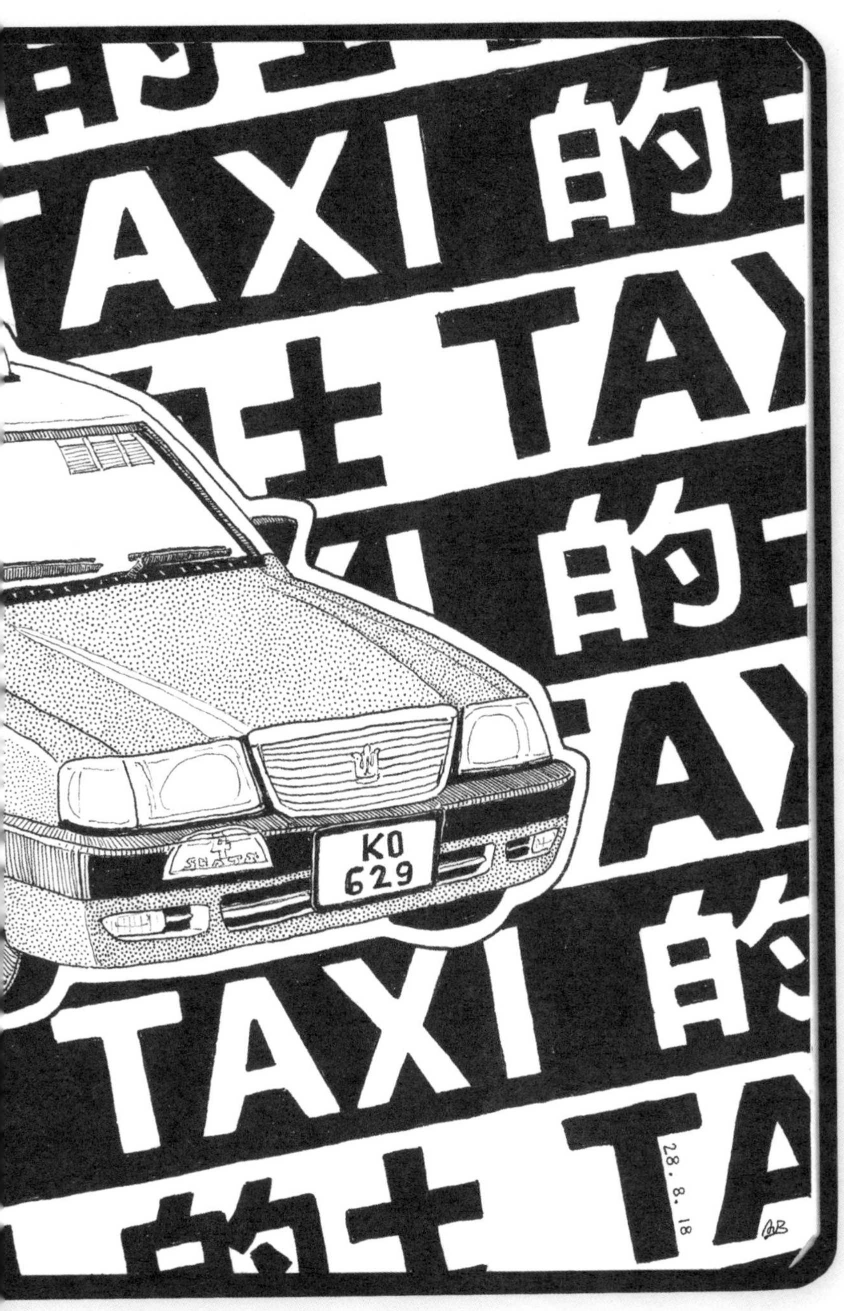

"Taxi" (2018)
Causeway Bay, Hong Kong

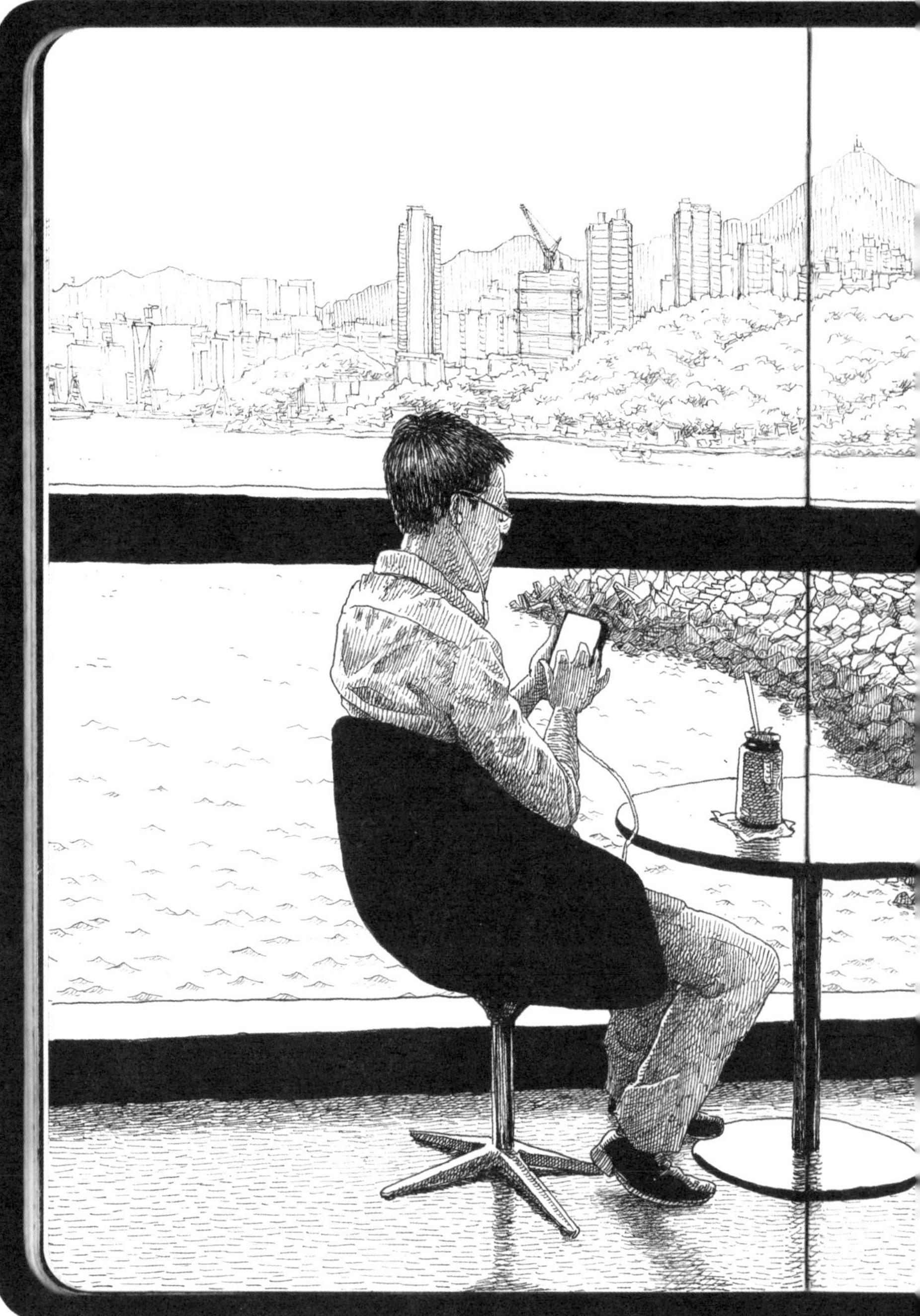

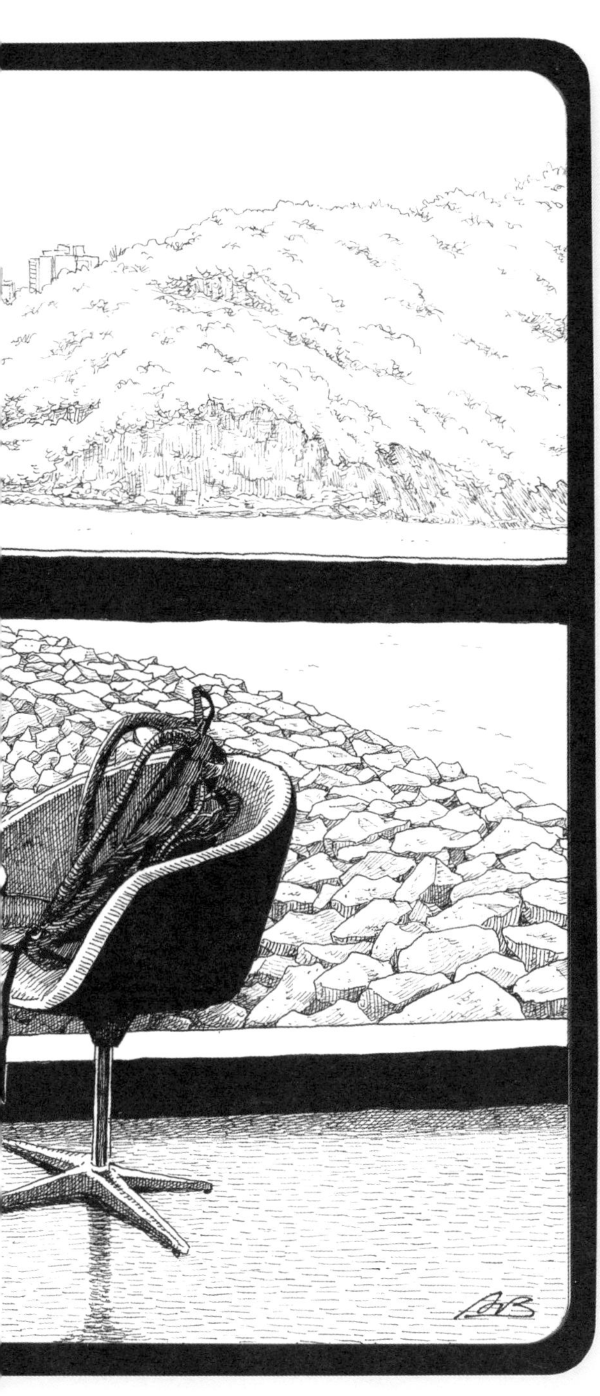

"Enjoying the View" (2021)
Chai Wan, Hong Kong

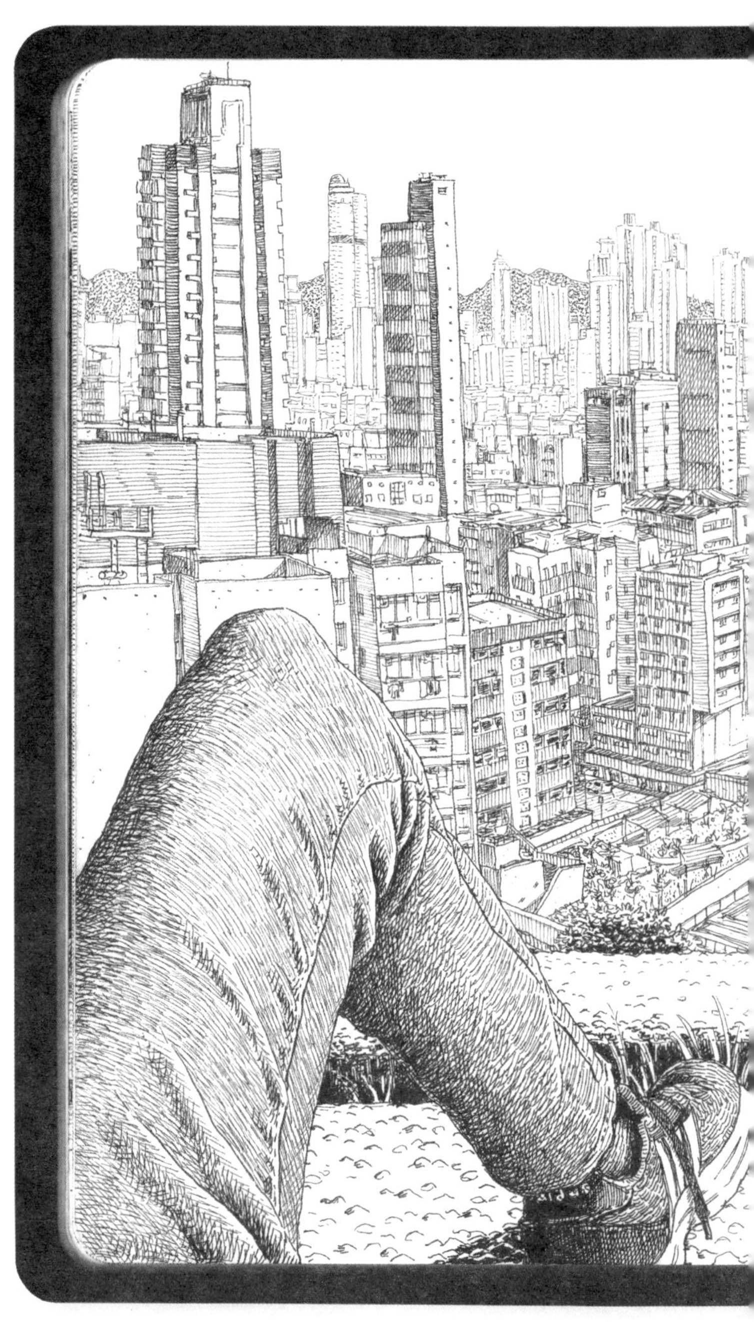

"Sham Shui Po, 2020" (2020)
Sham Shui Po, Hong Kong

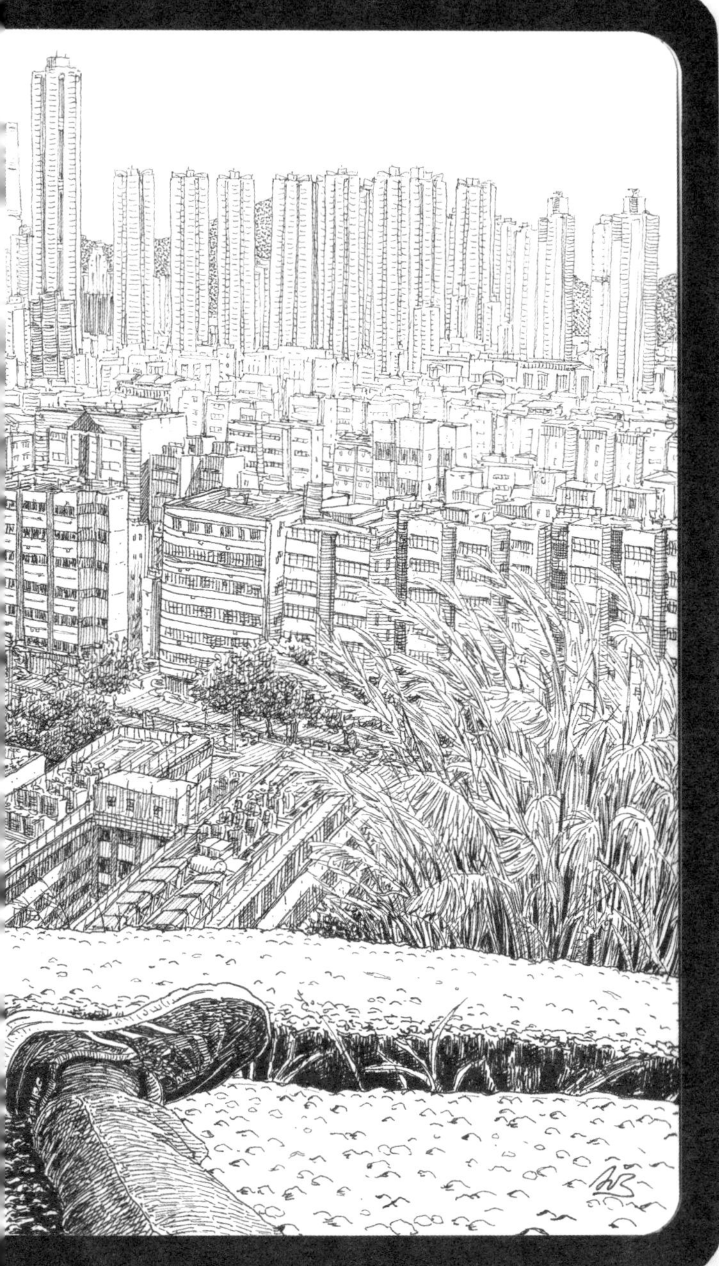

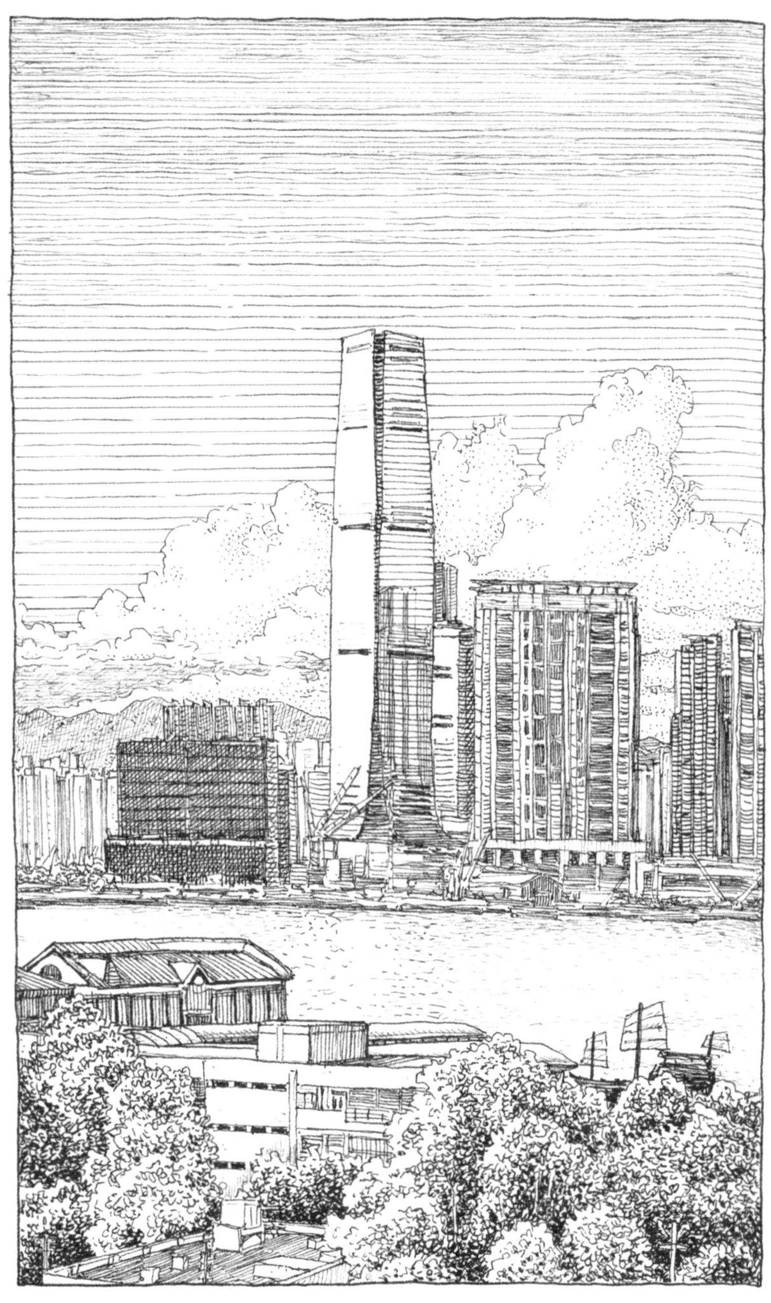

"ICC (from Lippo Centre)" (2021)
Admiralty, Hong Kong

“I don’t know where I’m going, but I’m on my way”

- Carl Sagan

CHAPTER II

MOTHER NATURE

As much as I adore Hong Kong as a city, part of its charm is its close proximity to nature. And that's something I've come to appreciate even more each year that I've been living here. The healing aspects of nature are just undeniable (especially for our minds), so when the bustling ambience of the city becomes a little bit too noisy and overwhelming, I find great comfort in walking down the easily accessible hiking trails that hide behind more or less every busy area.

As soon as I step onto that trail, something almost immediately changes in me. There's a tranquility there that simply can't be found on the crowded streets, and the further away I get from the sound of AC units and cars, that calm settles in further while transforming a simple "walk" into a journey of curious exploration. Eventually, new sounds will appear: the tussle of a bird jumping through the leafy vegetation in search of food, bamboo trees swaying in the wind high above, the trickle of a nearby forest stream and, occasionally, the heavy but quick steps of a boar (or several).

I like taking my backpack with me for most of these little trips into the forest. Aside from the obvious — my sketchbook and pens — I also tend to bring with me a thermos with tea or coffee and possibly a snack, depending on how long I plan on being out.

Right: ***"Infinity"*** (2021)
Braemar Hill, Hong Kong

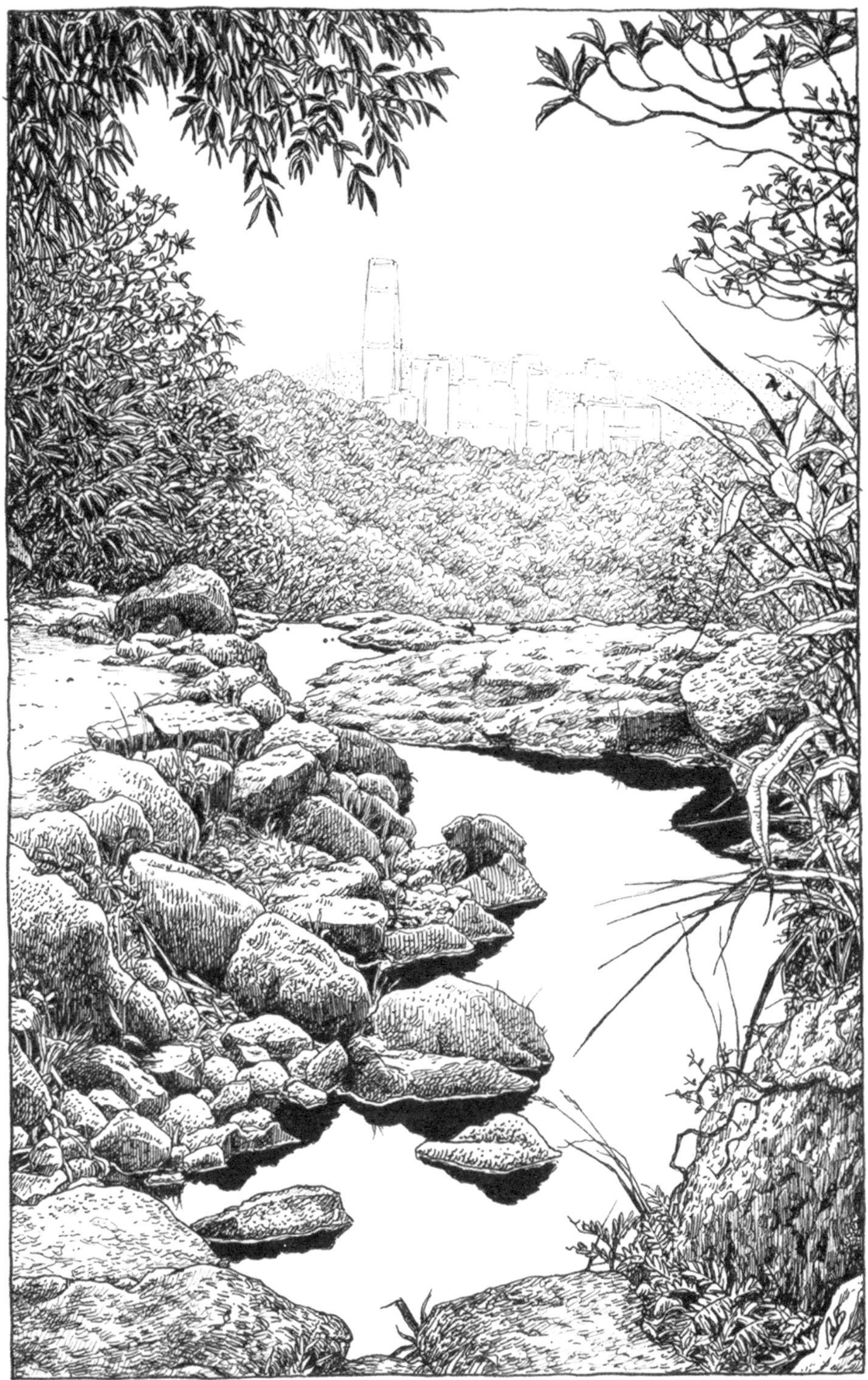

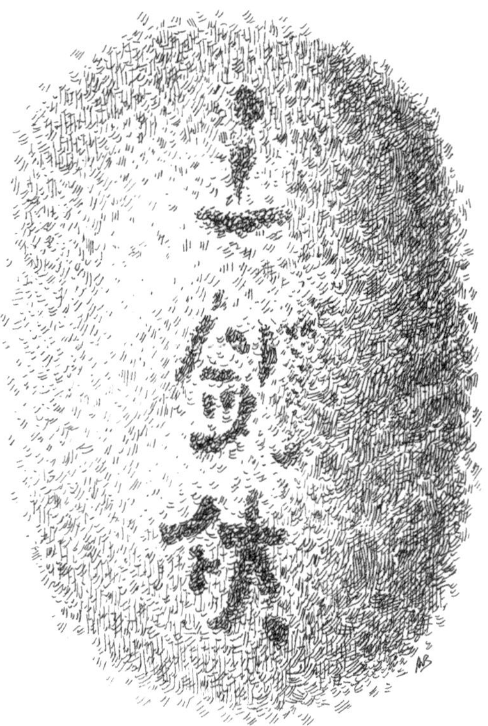

My bag also usually carries a set of binoculars, an old scarf for keeping the sweat away when it gets too hot (yes, I clean it) and, what might be the most essential item of them all: my trusted bottle of mosquito spray.

As you'll come to see when flipping through the pages in this particular chapter, several of my nature sketches tend to be made in close proximity to one another. That's because these places are found around the forests near my home. But, as you'll also discover, I have included several drawings from longer excursions to somewhat less accessible (but all the more fascinating and beautiful) spots around Hong Kong. Included in these are the magnificent views (don't just trust my drawings, go check them out for yourself!) from Kowloon Peak, the Wilson Trail and High Junk Peak, as well as darker and more cramped places, like the famous "Pirate Cave" on Cheung Chau.

Right: ***"Pirate Cave"*** (2021)
Cheung Chau, Hong Kong

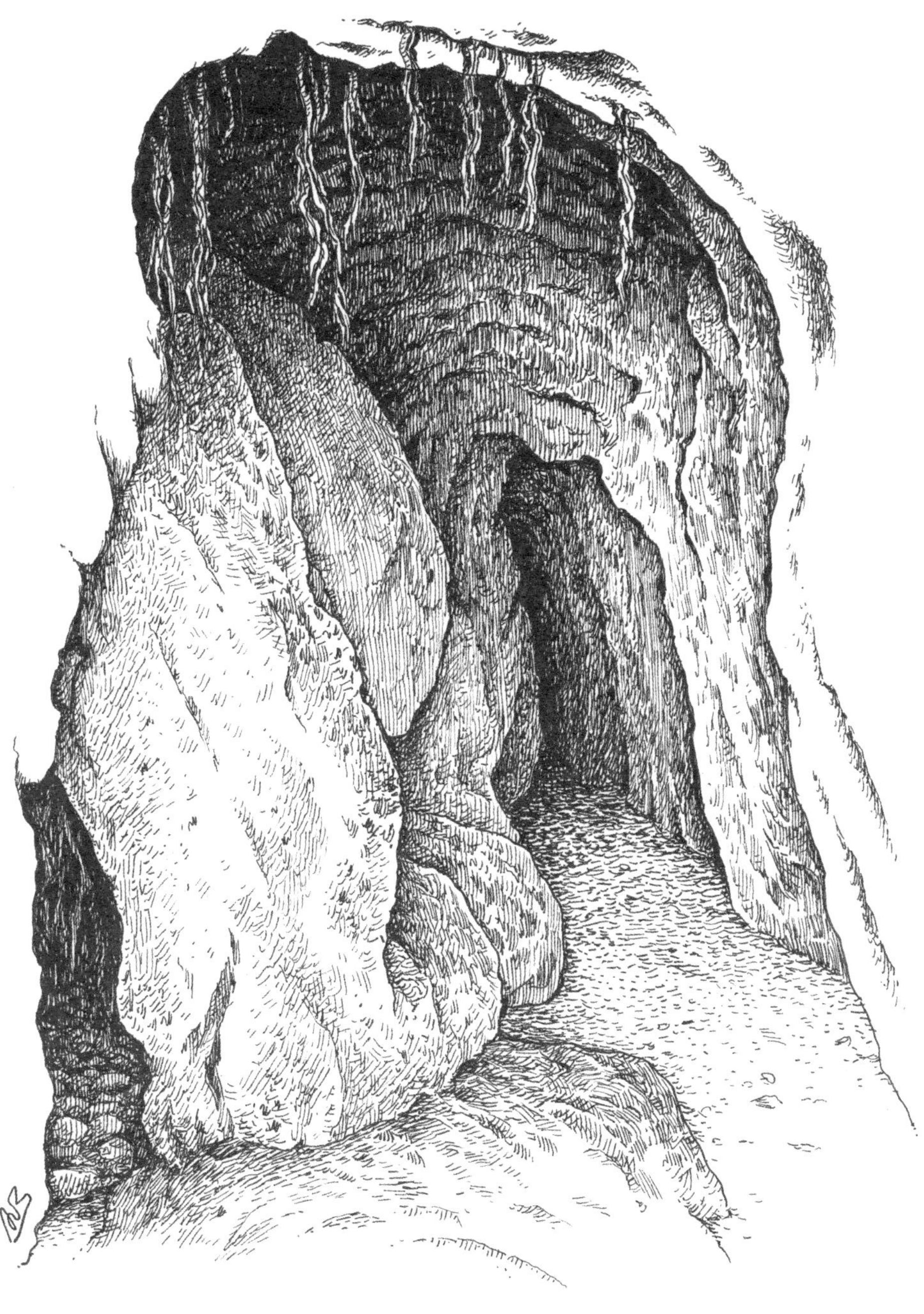

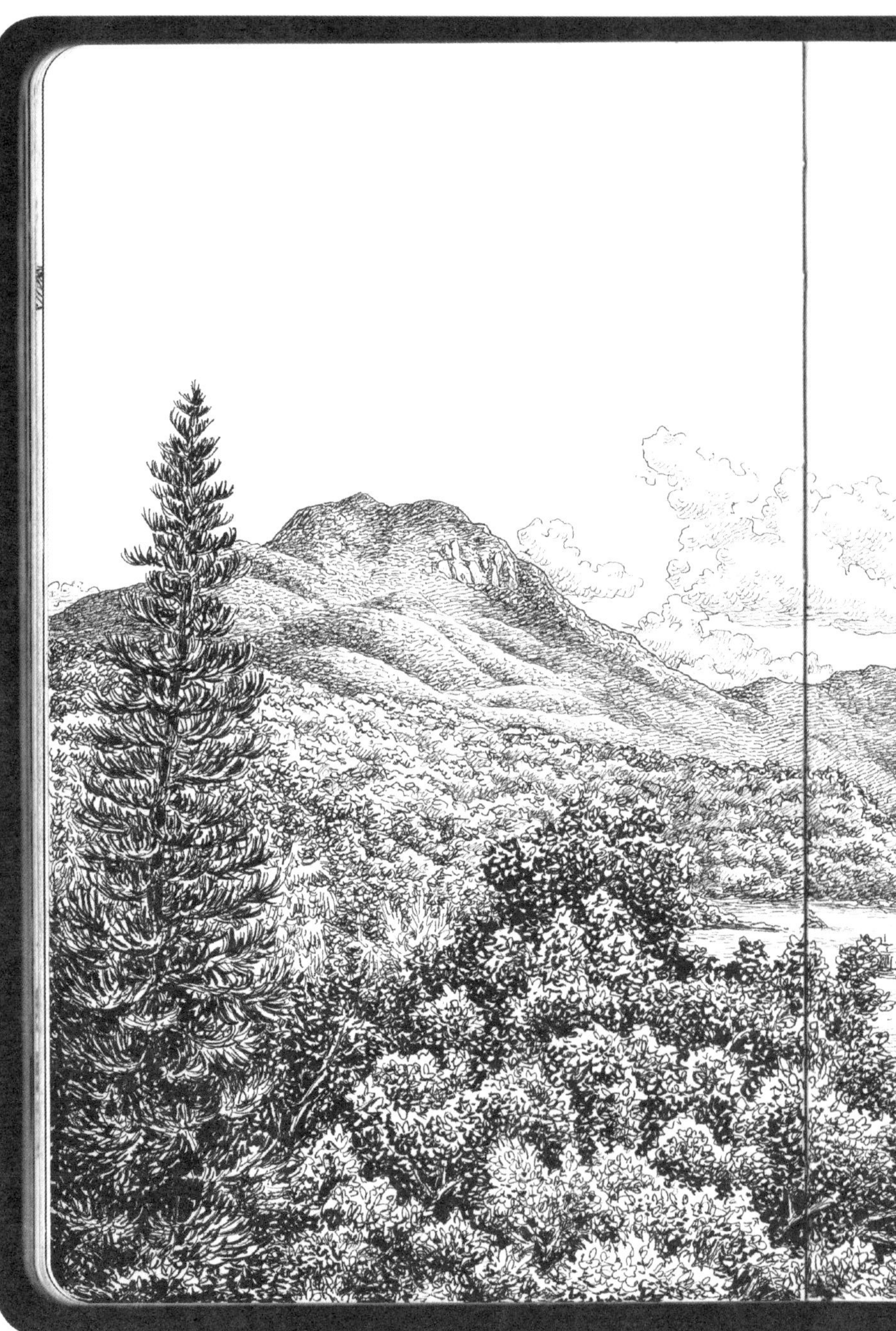

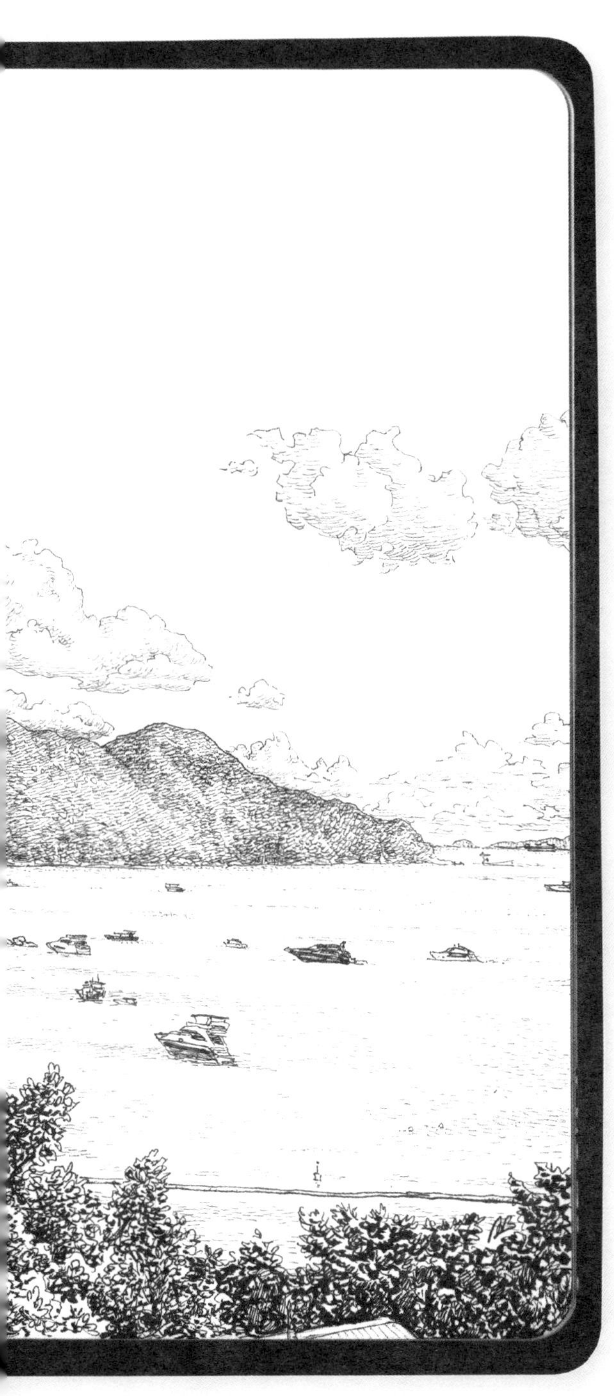

"Lamma" (2021)
Lamma Island, Hong Kong

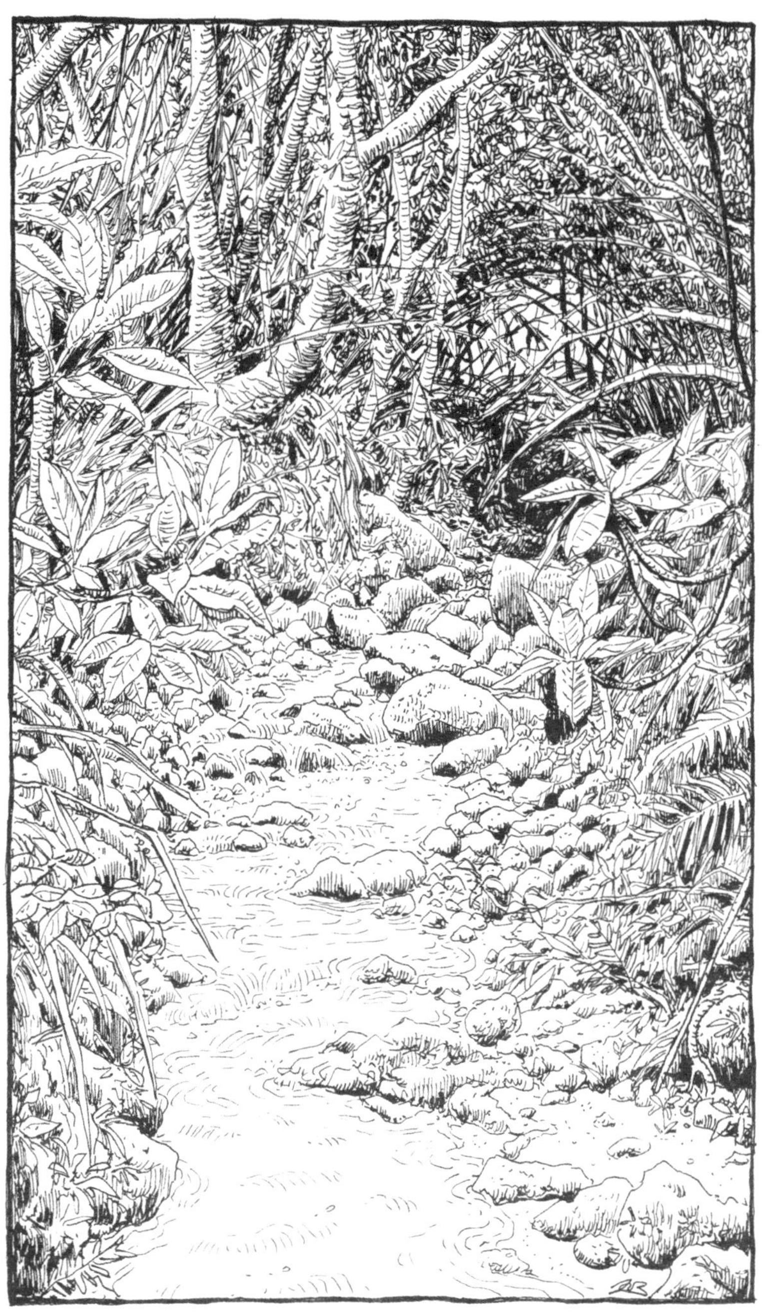

"Flow" (2019)
Braemar Hill, Hong Kong

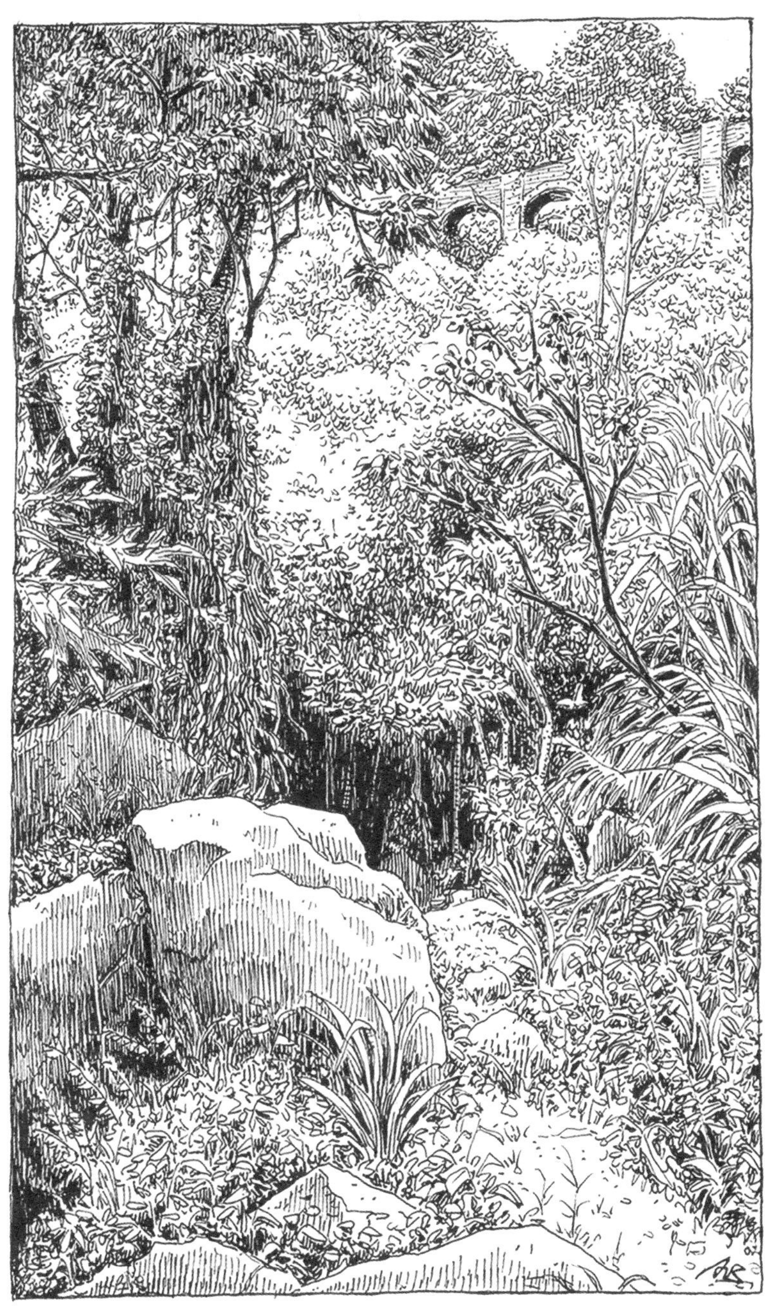

"The Explorer" (2019)
Happy Valley, Hong Kong

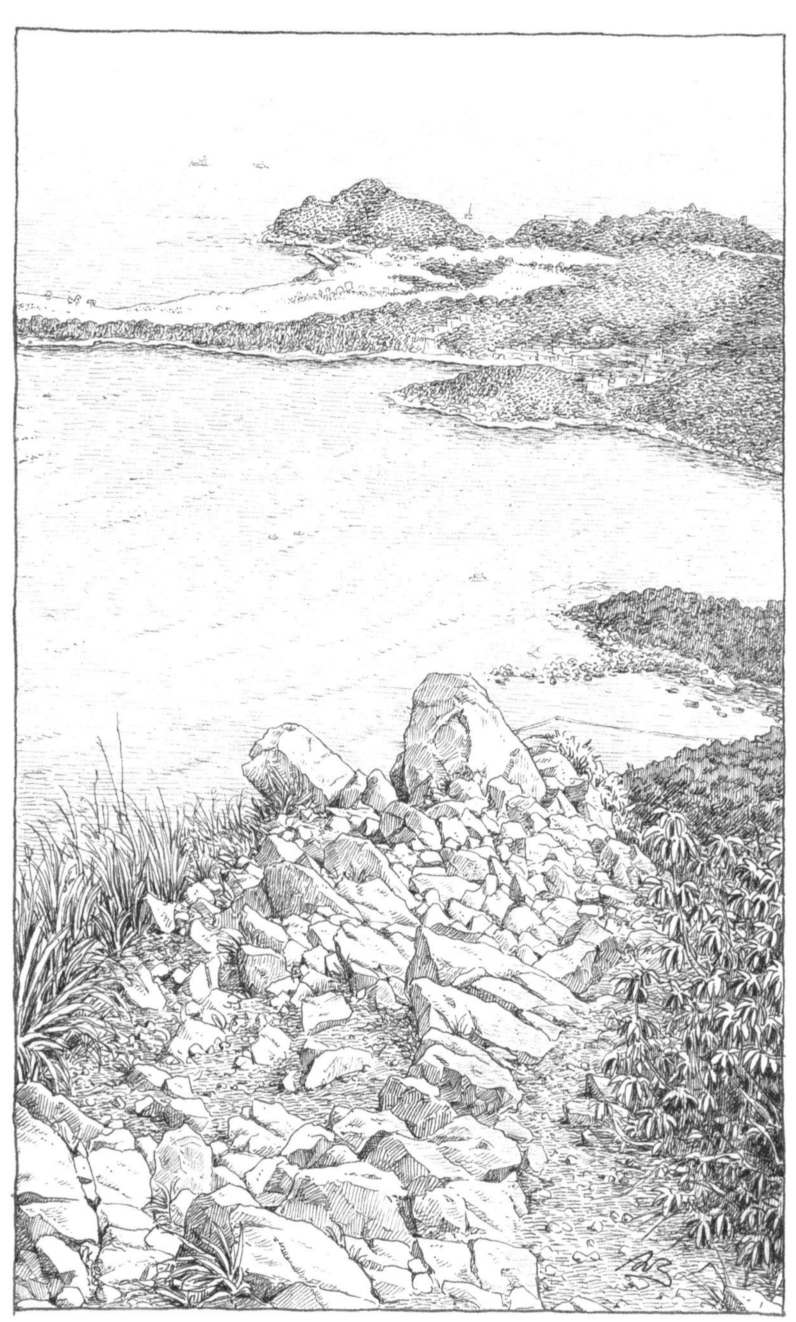

"High Junk Peak" (2022)
High Junk Peak, Hong Kong

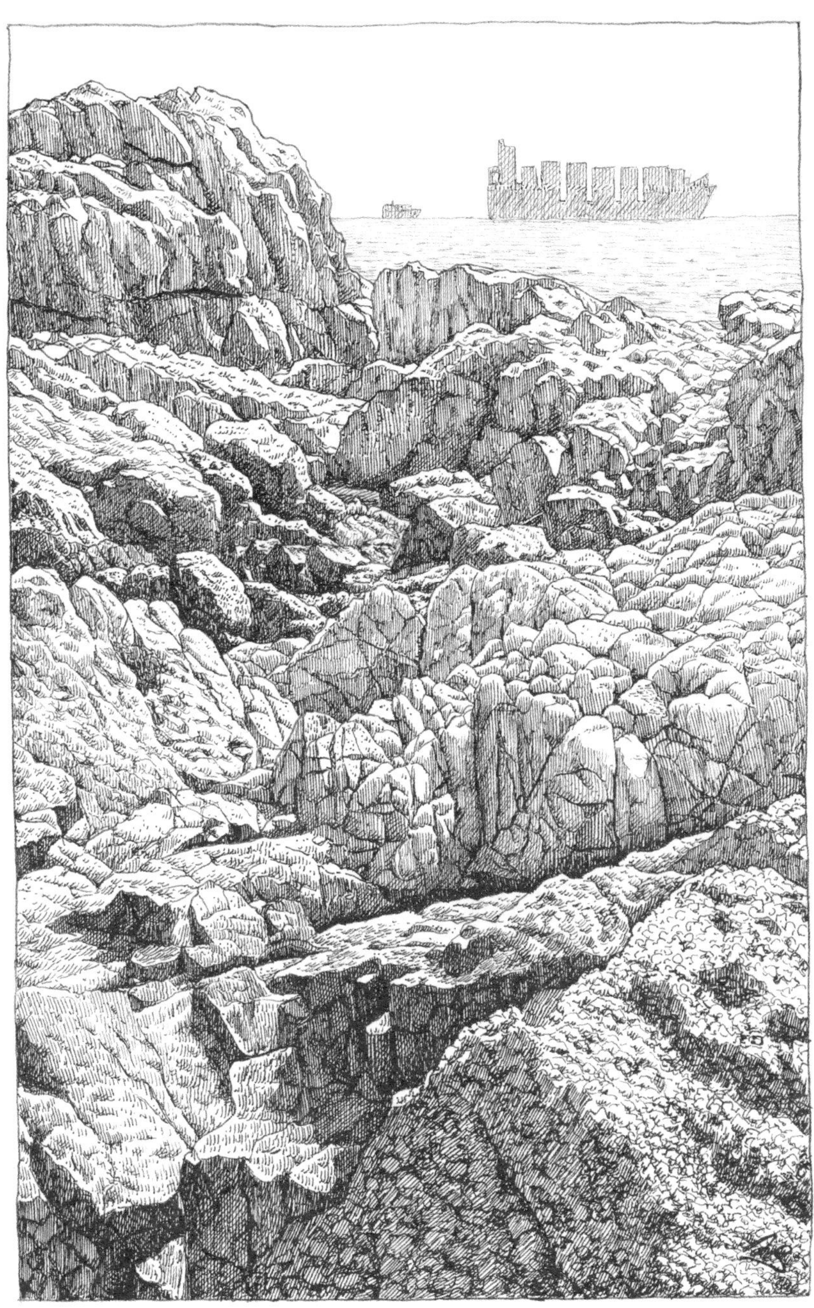

"Po Toi" (2022)
Po Toi, Hong Kong

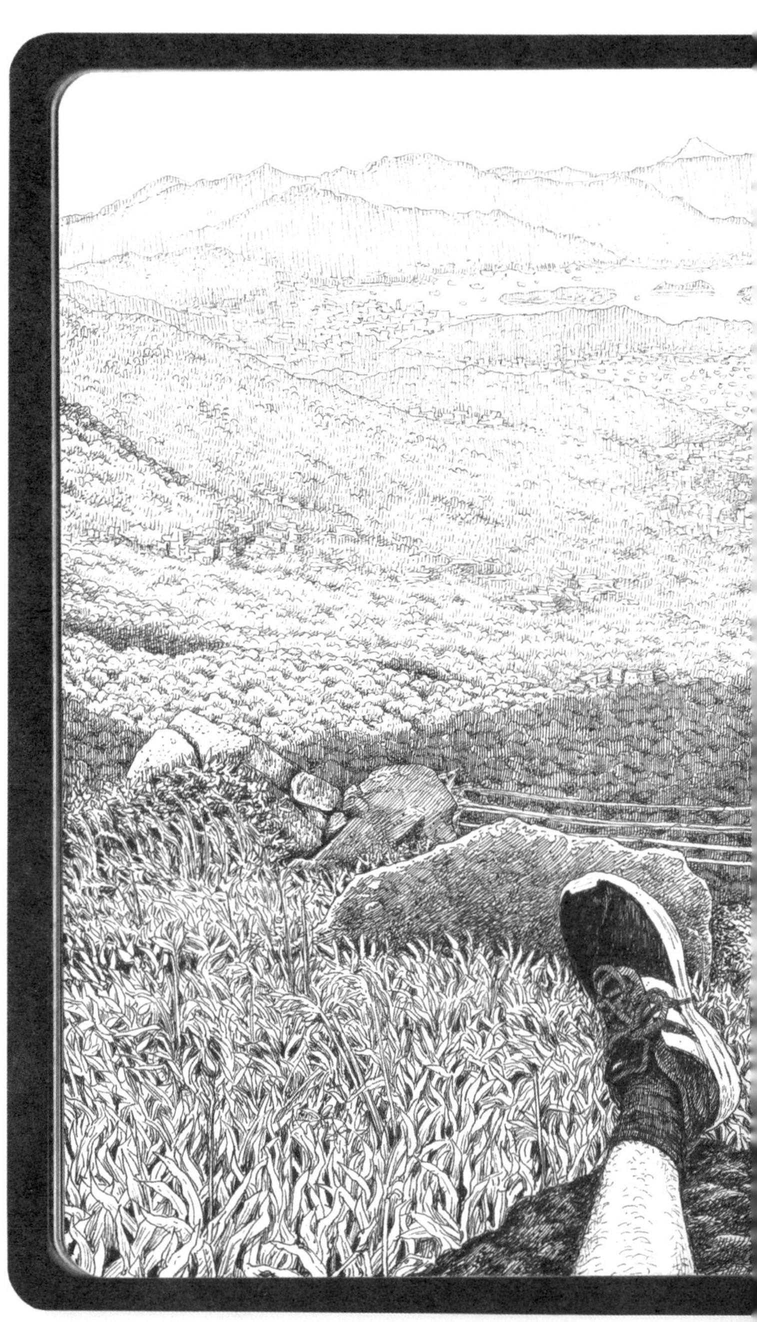

"Kowloon Peak" (2021)
New Kowloon, Hong Kong

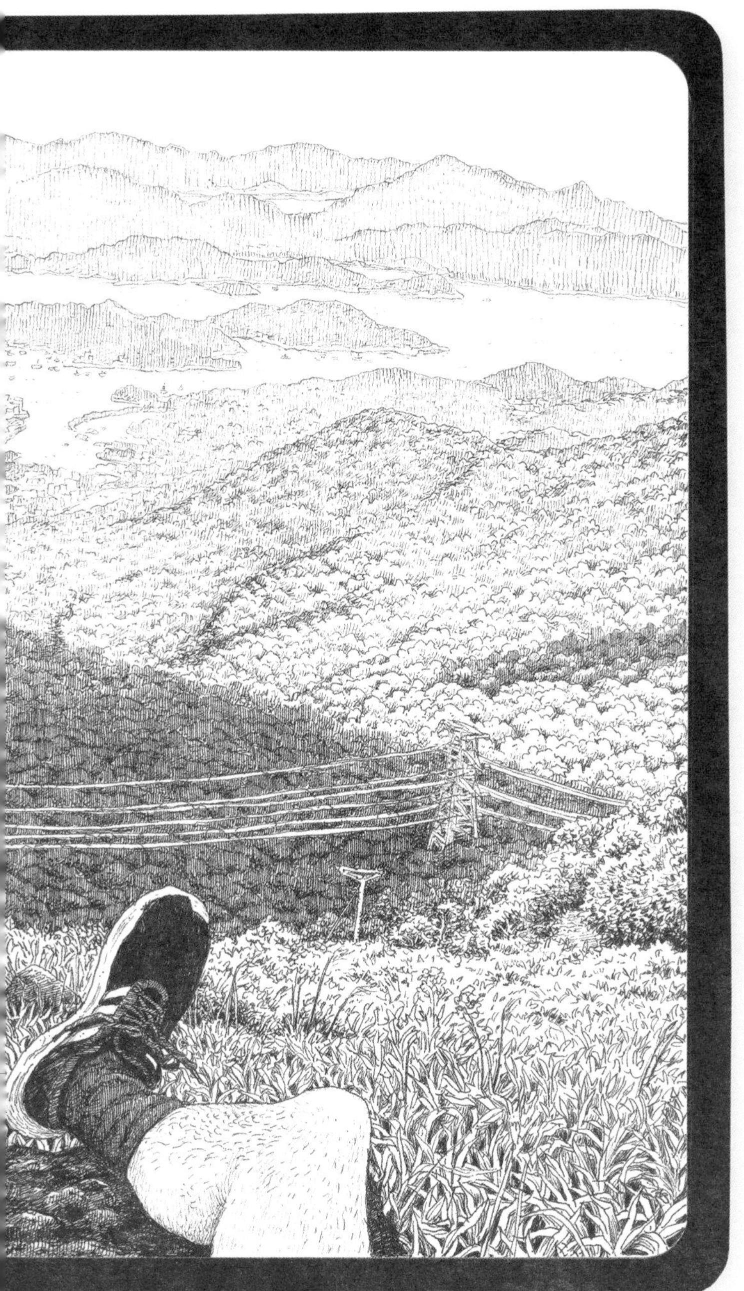

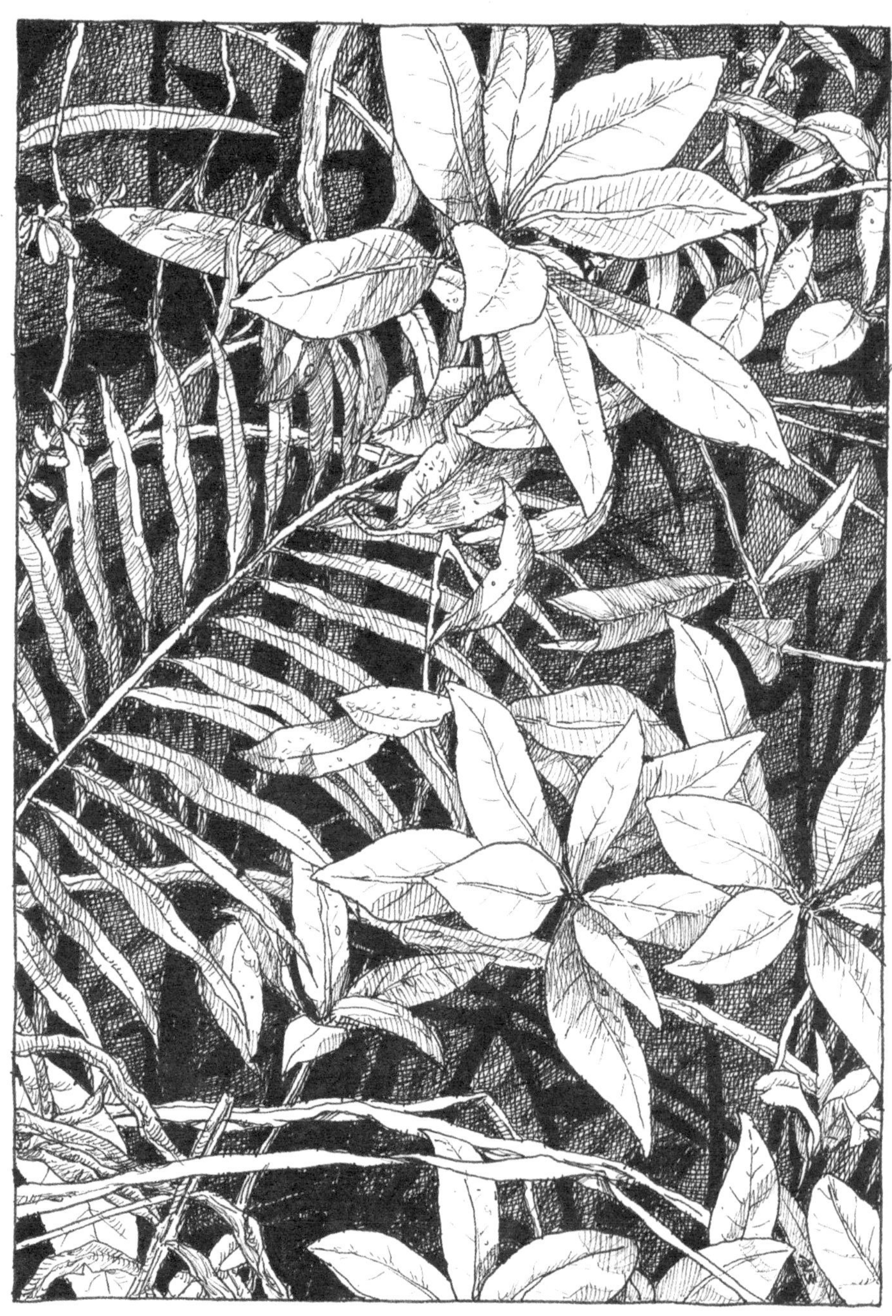

"Wilson Trail (Leaves)" (2021)
Yau Tong, Hong Kong

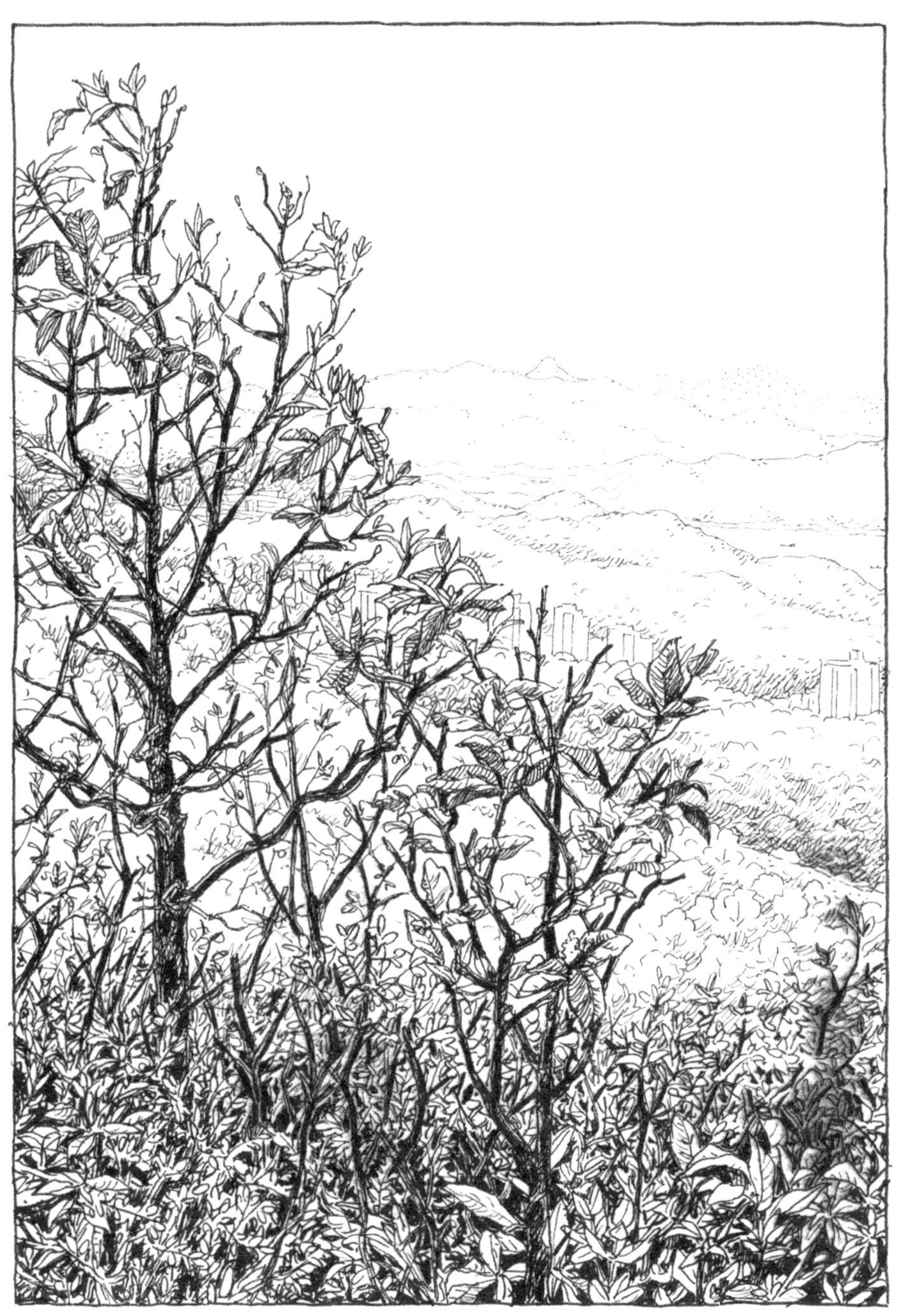

"Wilson Trail (View)" (2021)
Yau Tong, Hong Kong

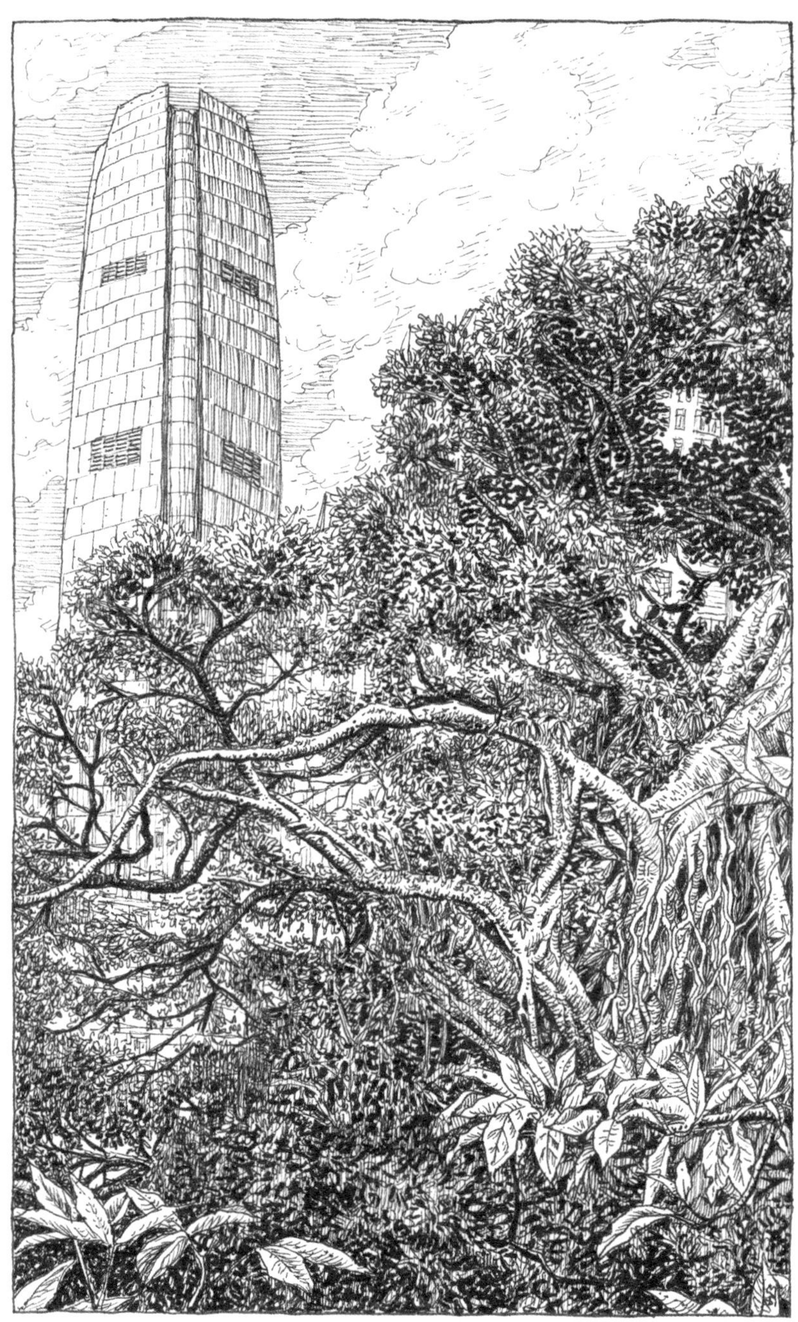

"Looming" (2020)
Quarry Bay, Hong Kong

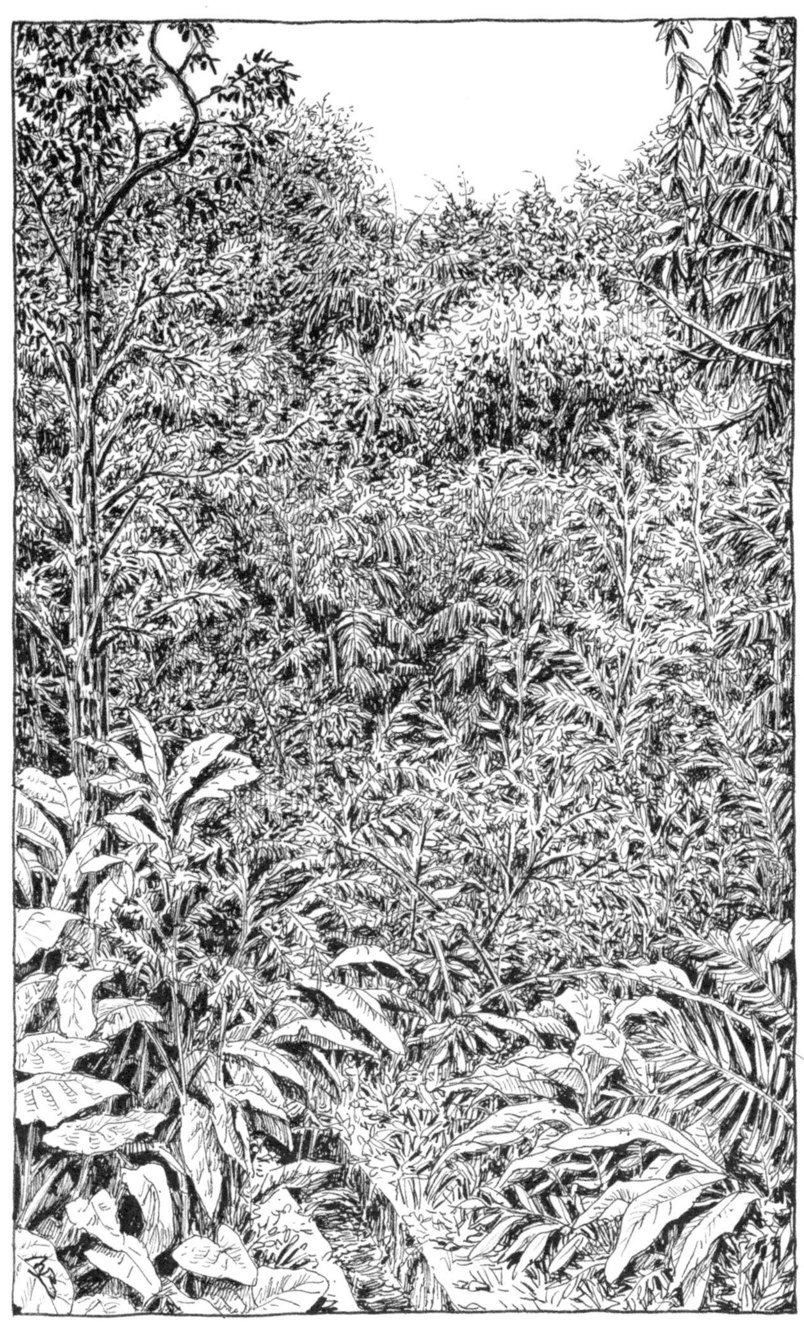

"Listen" (2020)
Quarry Bay, Hong Kong

As city-dwellers, it's often easy to forget the immense power of the very nature that surrounds us. That is, of course, until the next typhoon hits. In October of 2018 Hong Kong was hit with the worst typhoon that I have ever experienced during my near-decade in this city. Classified as a "T10", Mangkhut was a storm to avoid at all costs, and it goes without saying that people were advised to stay indoors. Naturally, schools and workplaces were temporarily closed.

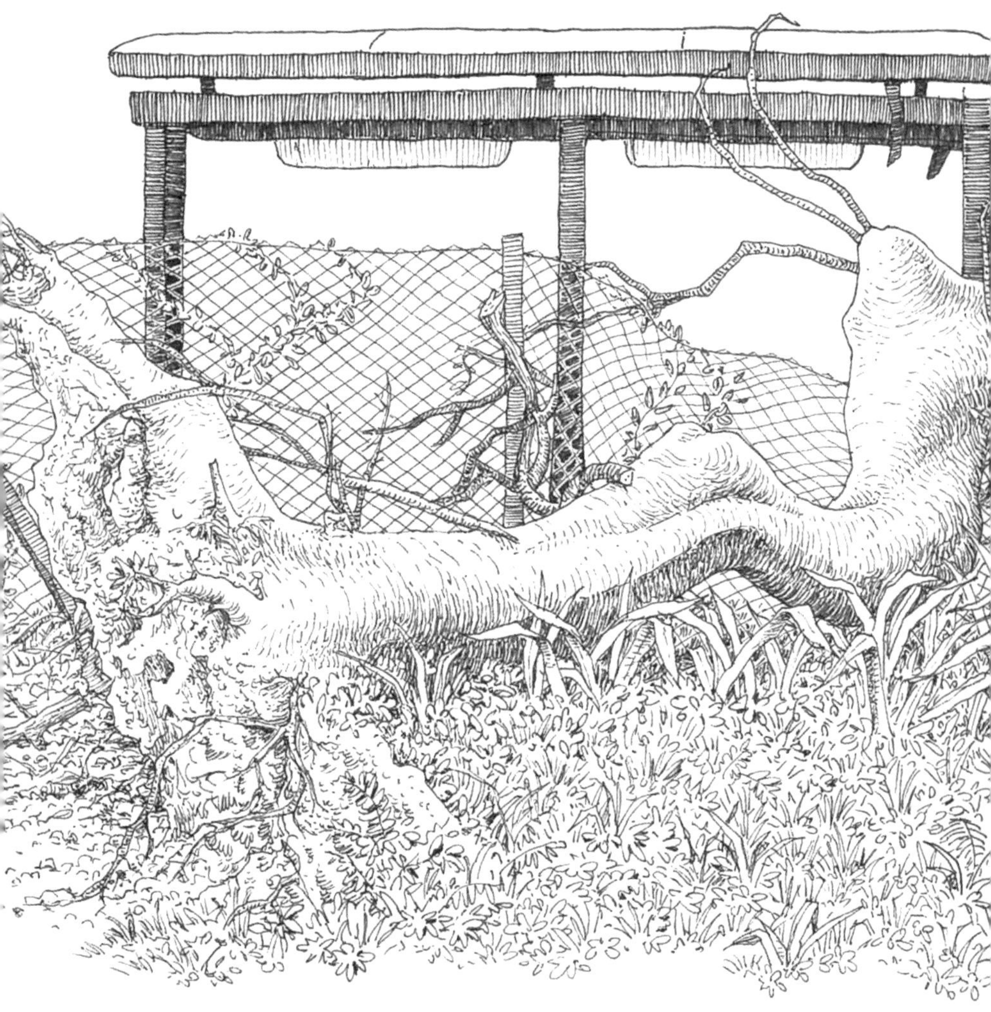

Other than the short amount of time I spent outside on the street sketching (not advisable whatsoever), most of the devastation caused by the storm was for me seen either online or in the disruptive aftermath.

It should be pointed out here that Hong Kong was by no means hit as bad as some other places, like the Philippines, though fallen trees and other debris did still cause a bit of trouble once the storm had passed: like this fallen giant in Braemar Hill, which had tipped over a sports ground fence.

"Fallen Giant" (2018)
Braemar Hill, Hong Kong

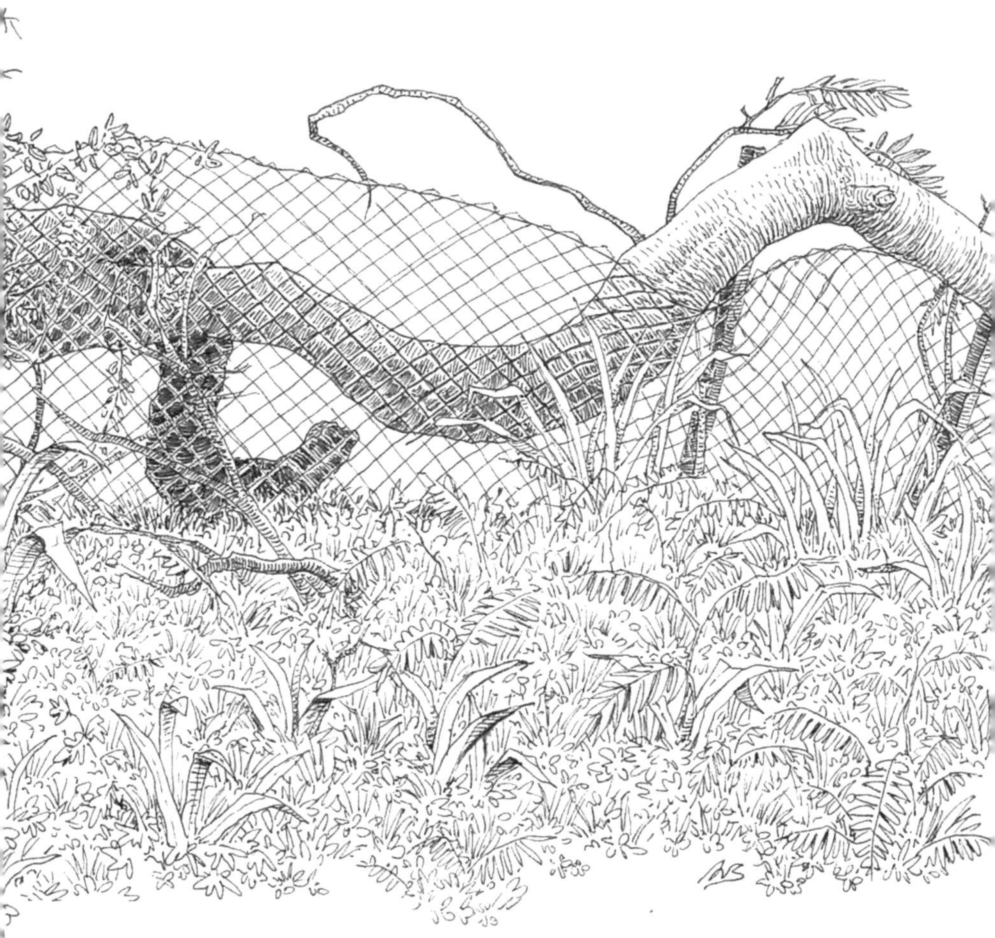

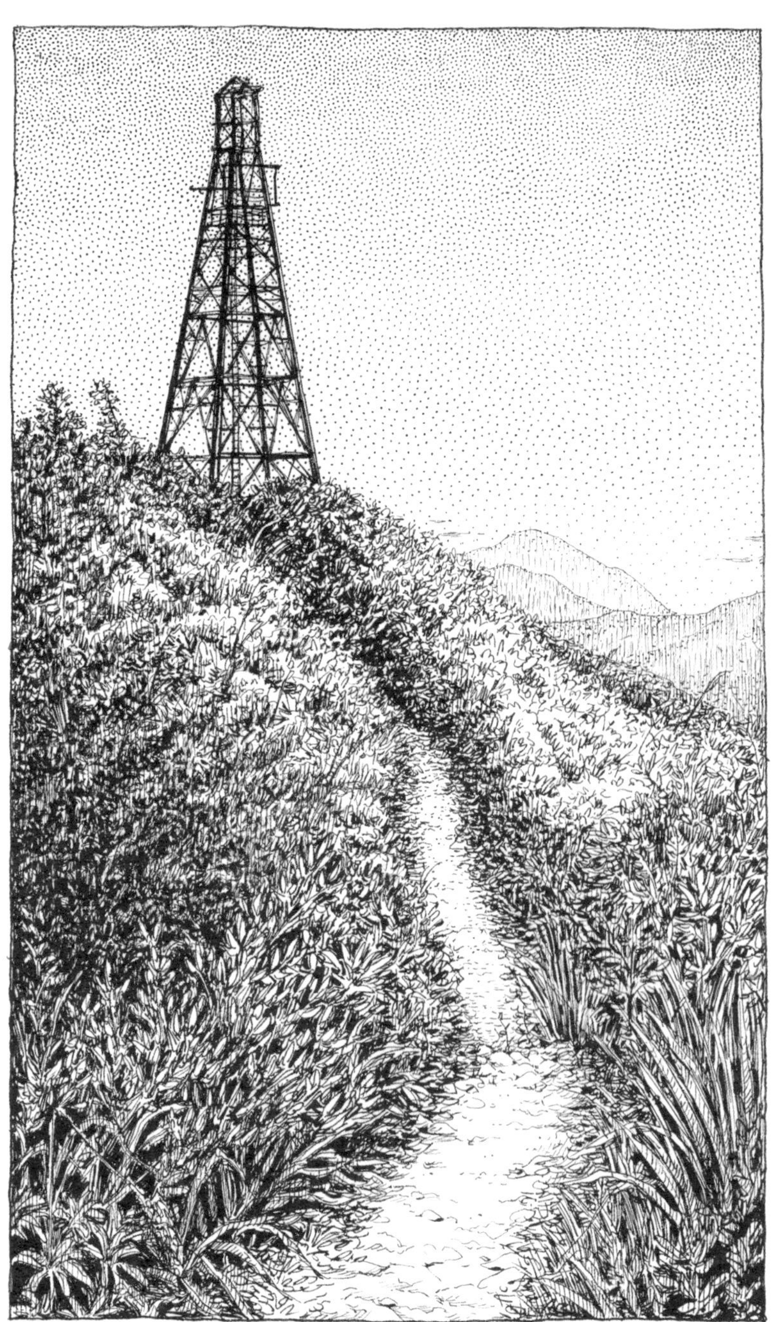

"On My Way" (2019)
Mount Butler, Hong Kong

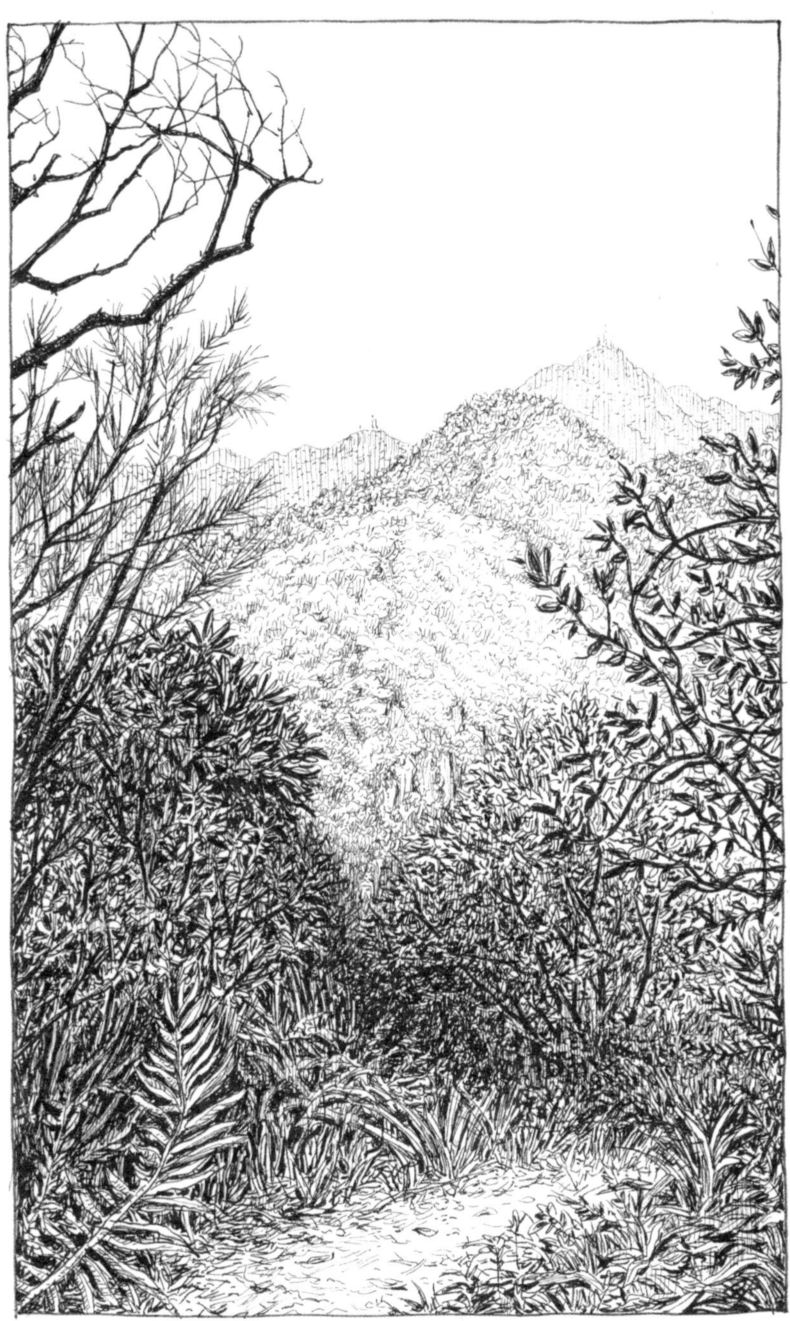

"Those Who Wander" (2020)
Yau Tong, Hong Kong

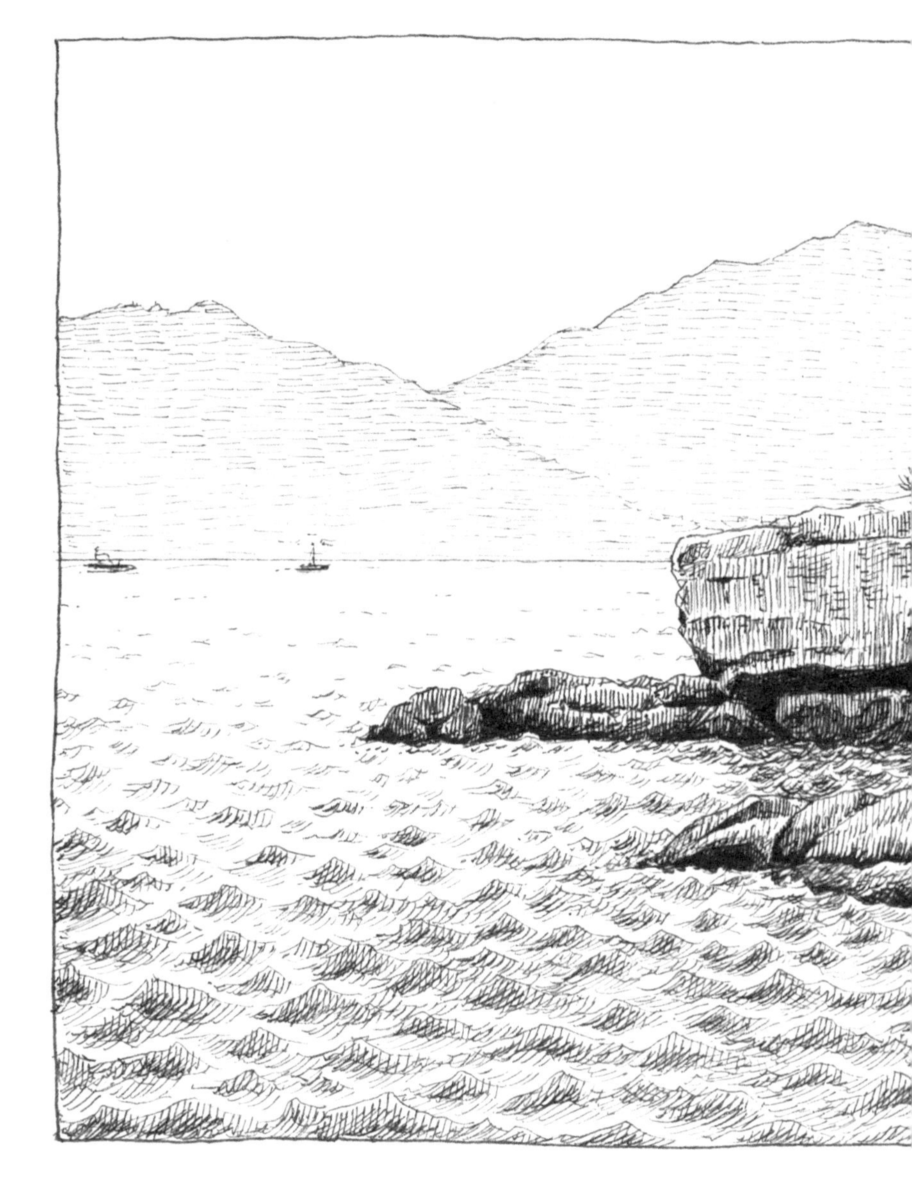

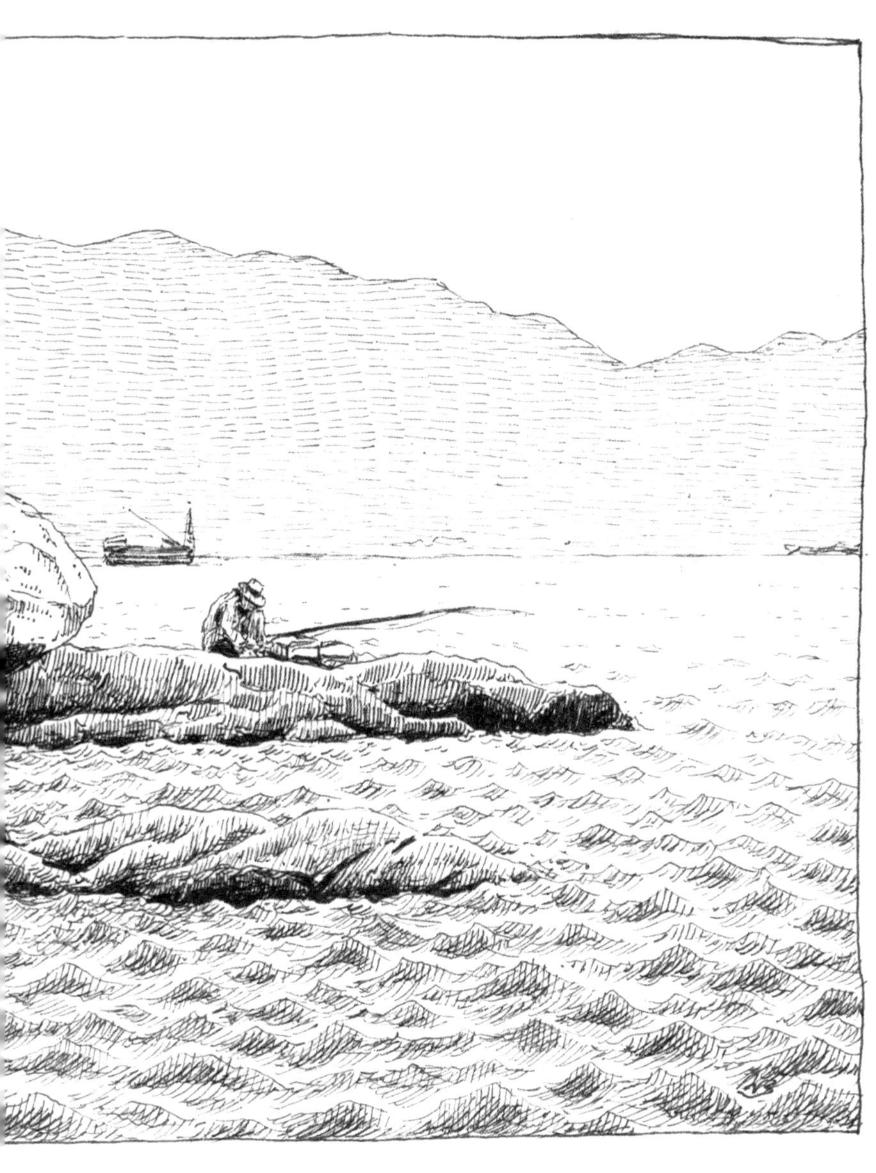

"Fishing" (2020)
Gold Coast, Hong Kong

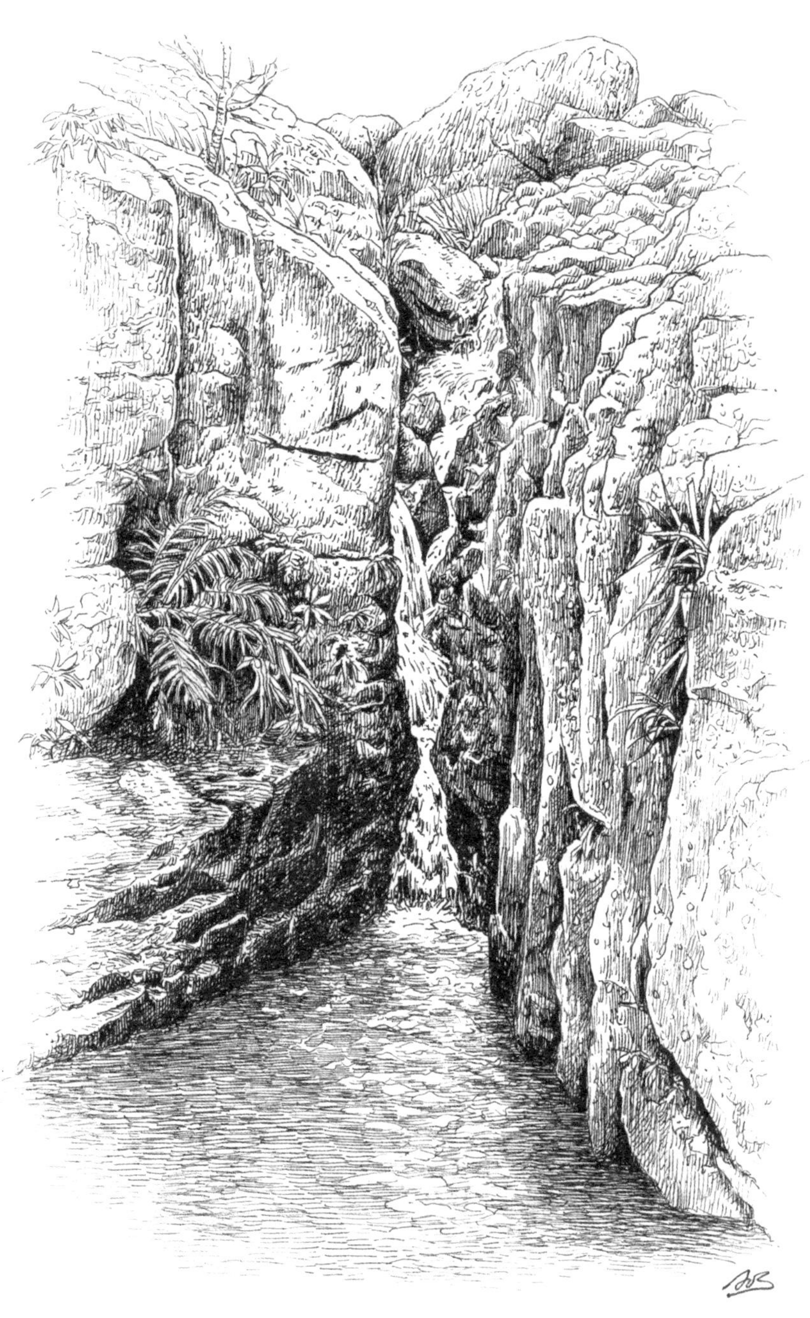

"Waterfall" (2021)
Braemar Hill, Hong Kong

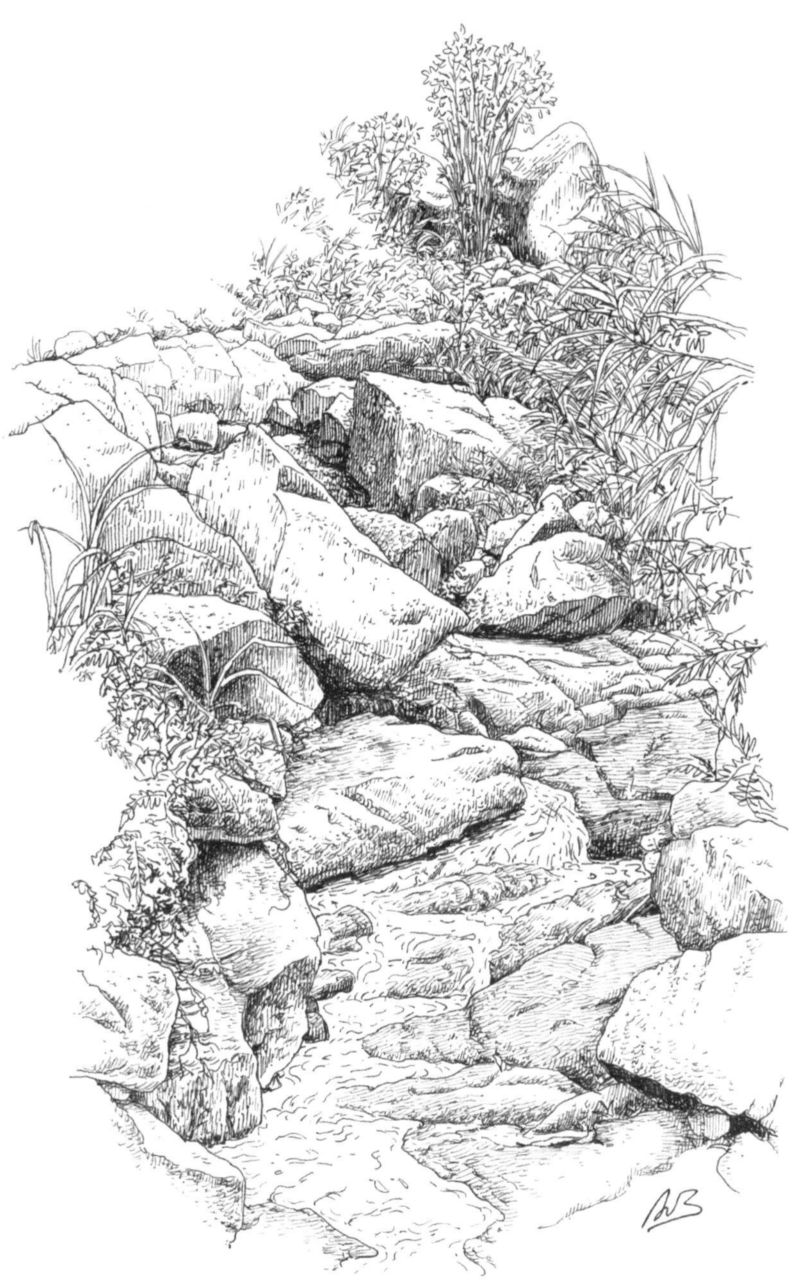

"Stream" (2021)
Braemar Hill, Hong Kong

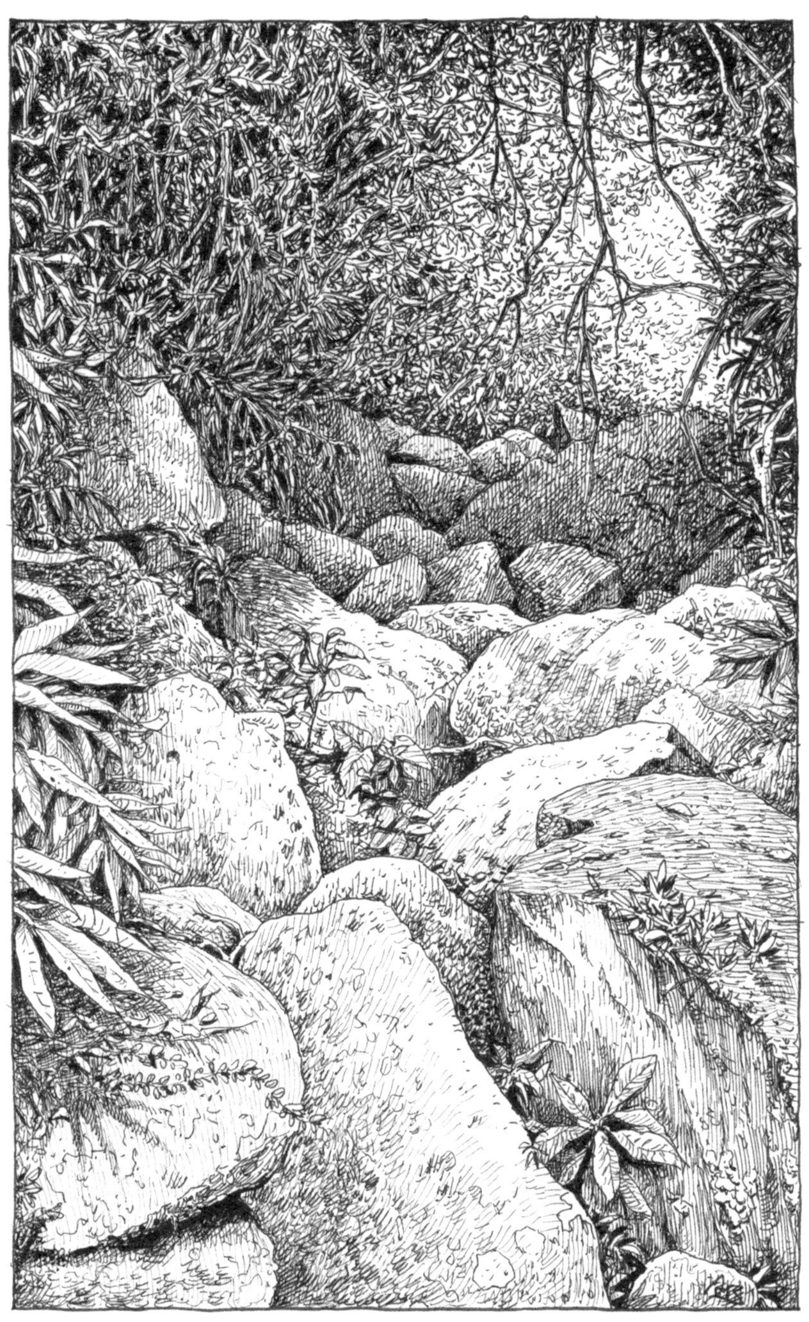

"Boulders" (2020)
Braemar Hill, Hong Kong

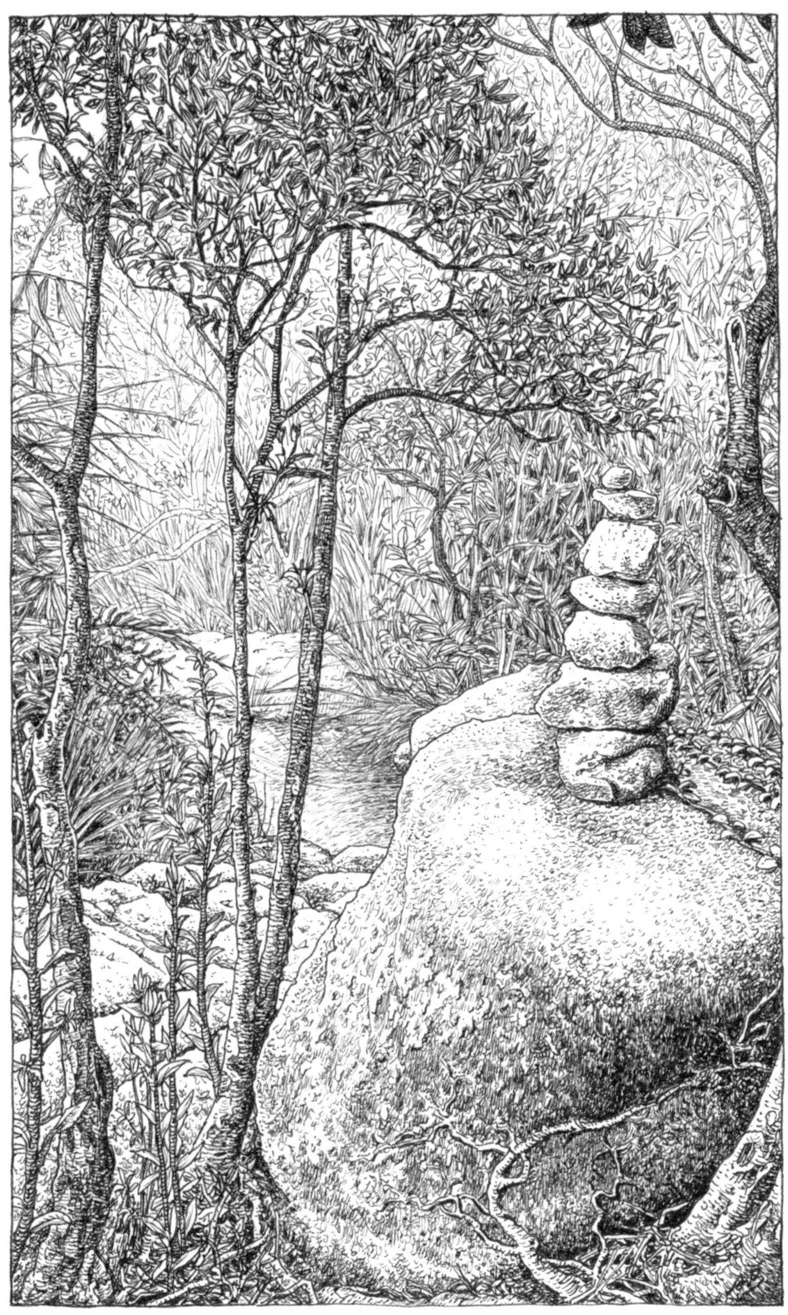

"Secret Spot (2022)
Braemar Hill, Hong Kong

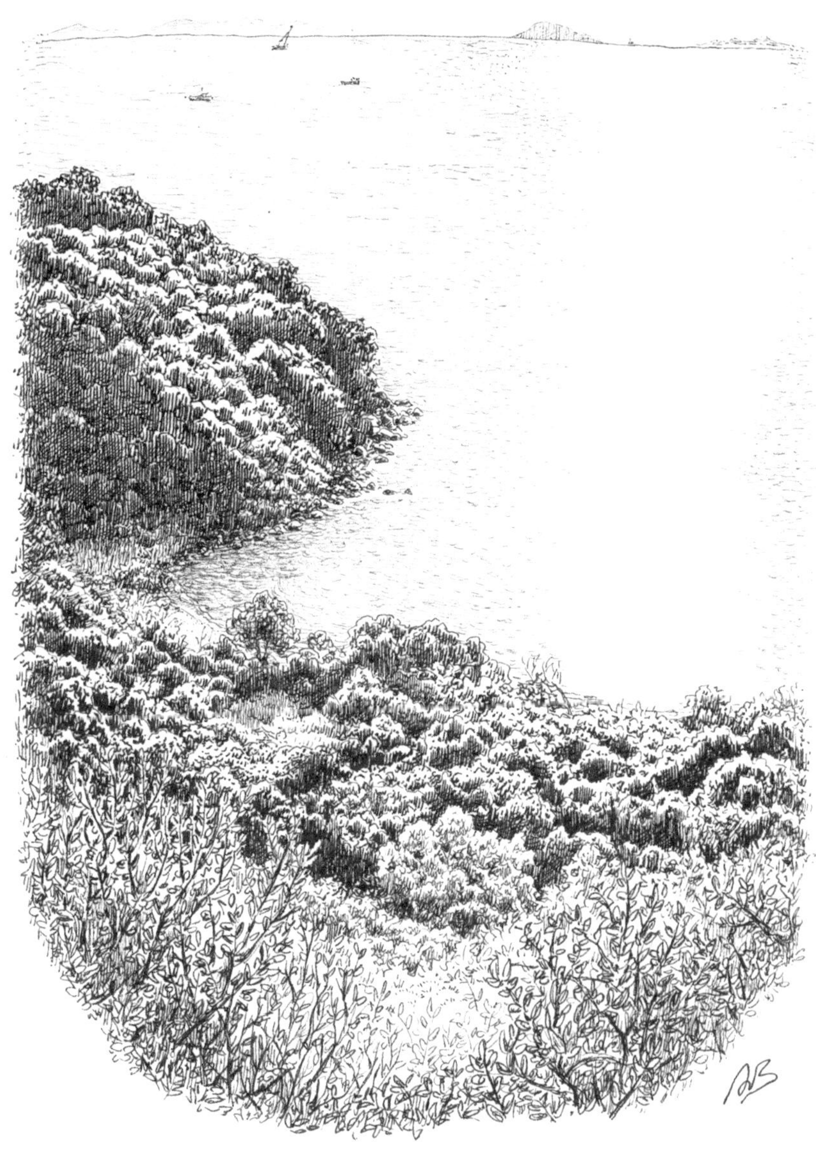

"Lamma Sunset" (2022)
Lamma Island, Hong Kong

" I just need some time in a beautiful place to clear my head "

- J.R.R. Tolkien

CHAPTER III

FADED MEMORIES

"Time devours all things". One of my favorite aspects of Hong Kong is something that I think many people overlook: all of the old structures that have long since been handed over to nature. From old military outposts in Yau Tong to apartment buildings to abandoned motorbikes, part of Hong Kong's rich history can be found in things forgotten.

Sometimes, I've ventured out to specific spots that I've read about online. Other times, I've simply stumbled upon them during my usual hikes or walks around the city. I think what fascinates me about these things devoured by time is just that: the reminder that time is a constant force in our lives and nothing escapes it. It's like a "Memento Mori" (think old paintings of human skulls, clocks, rotten fruit and other reminders of the fleeting nature of life) on the side of the road. Likewise, it's a testament to the power of Mother Nature and it's showing how quickly she will reclaim her territory once we stop "fighting" her.

Aside from the aforementioned aspect of these historical subjects, I should also mention my second reason for loving to draw these sites and sceneries: the sheer sense of mystery and adventure that I feel when looking upon them (please excuse me while I "geek out" for a moment).

Right: ***"Quiet Ruins"*** (2019)
Yau Tong, Hong Kong

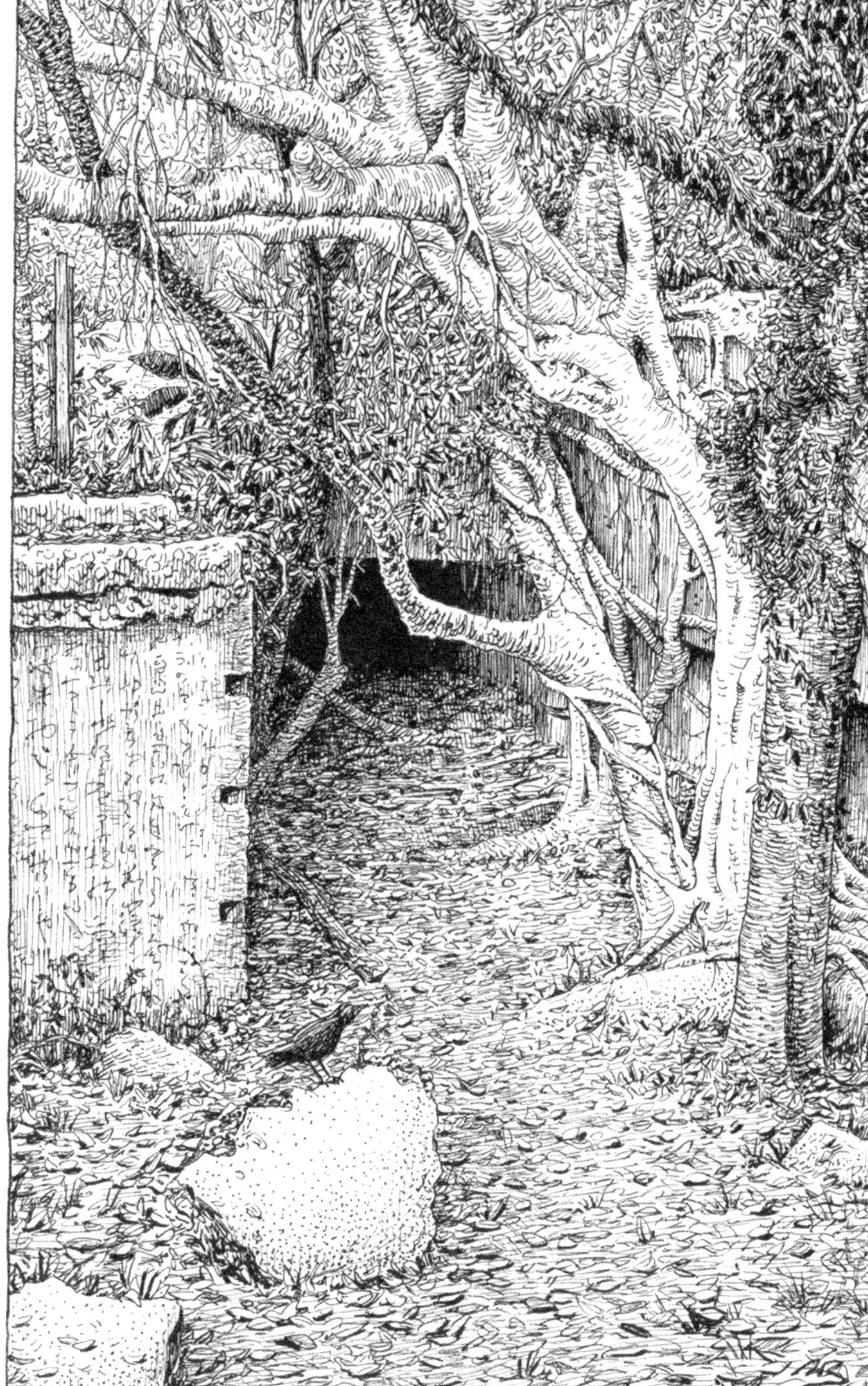

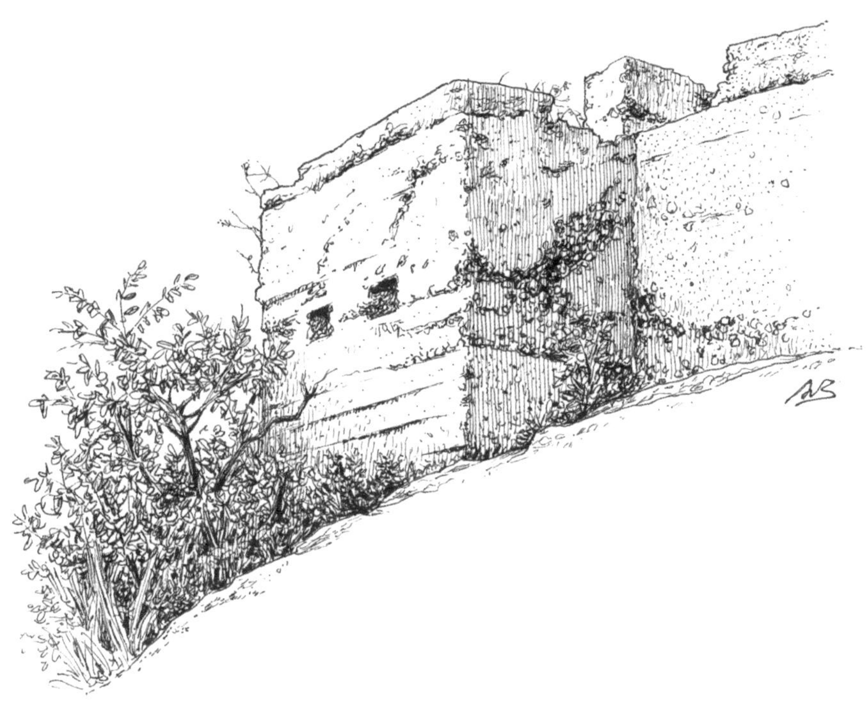

I've long been a fan of books, movies and video games such as "The Lord of the Rings" trilogy, "Indiana Jones", "Tomb Raider" and "Uncharted" (just to name a few), and I think this comes from the joy of discovering and exploring places and things from the past, whether decades, centuries or millennia old. When looking upon these sites, I almost feel like I'm transported into a storybook or some other work of mysterious fiction, and it's this very notion that I want to convey when depicting them. I can only hope that you, the viewer, are left with a similar feeling.

Right: ***"Remnants"*** (2021)
Yau Tong, Hong Kong

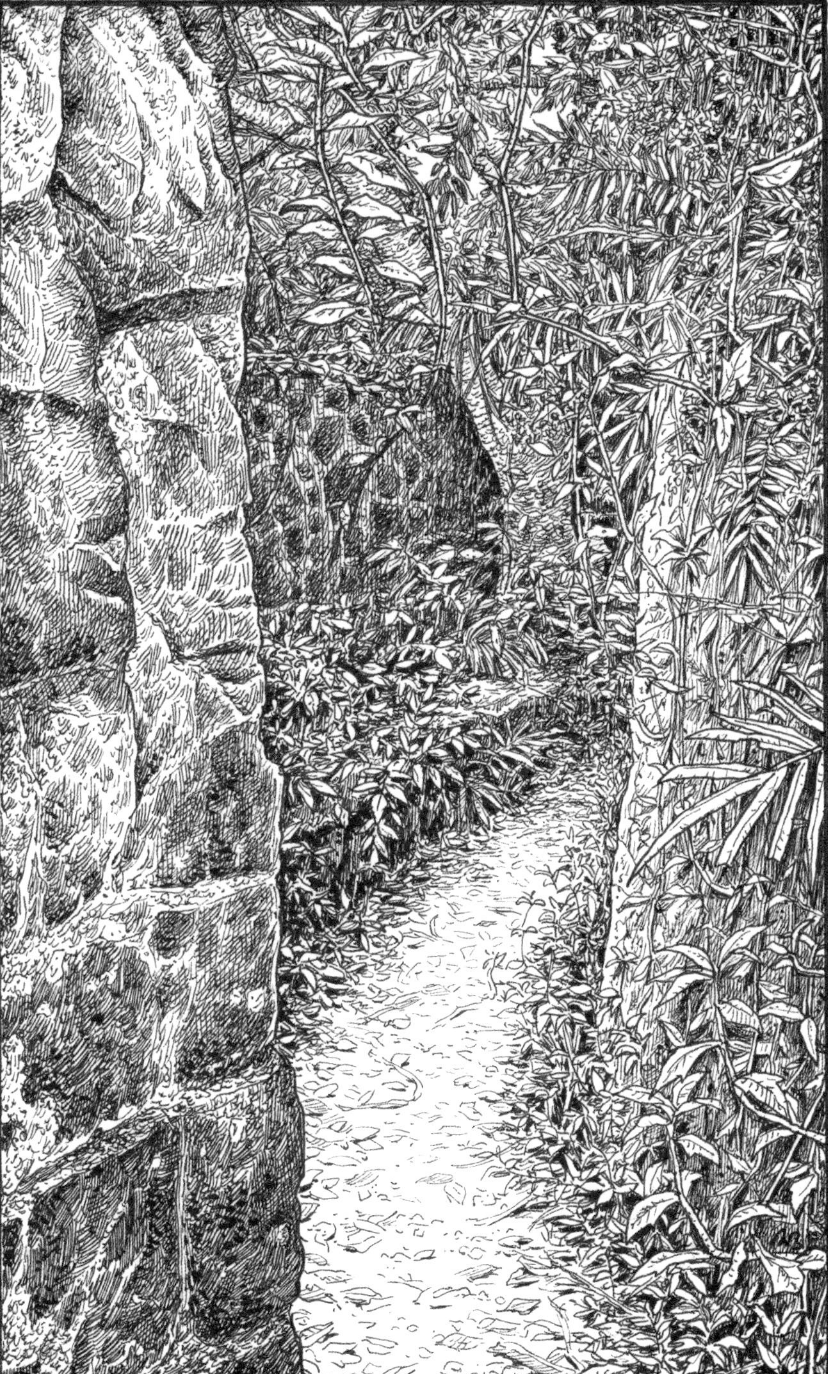

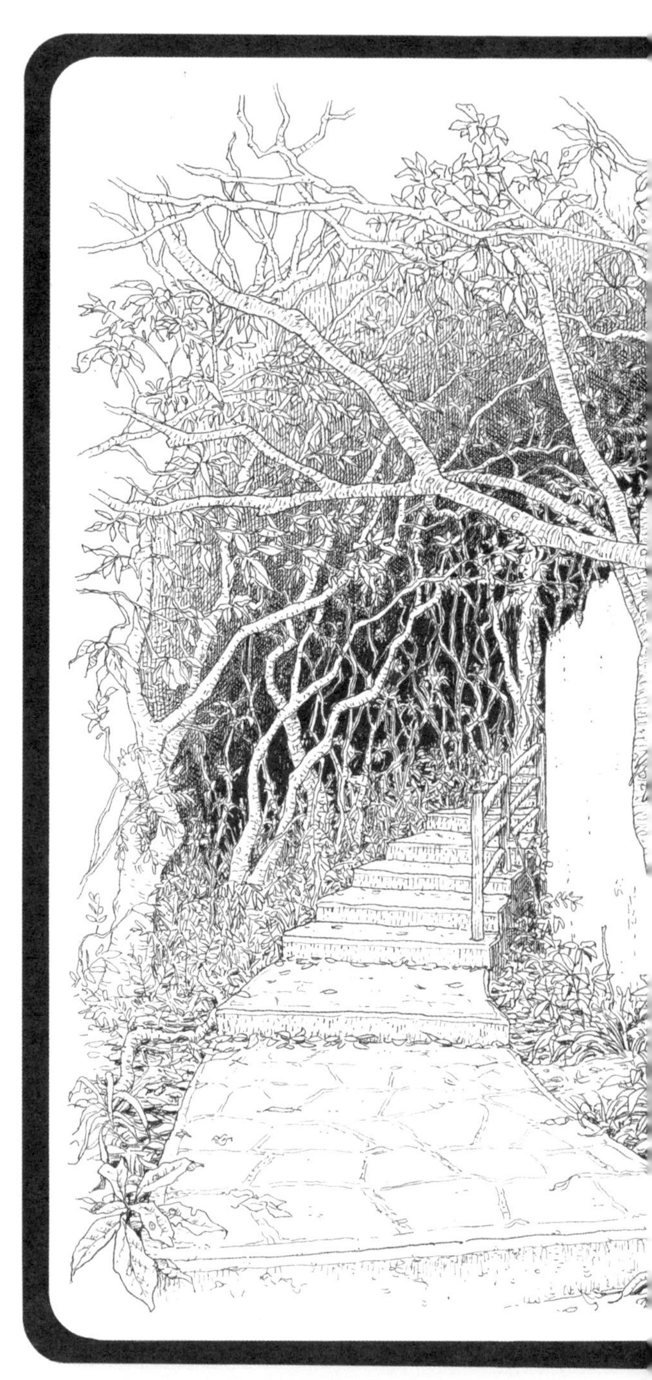

"Forest Ruin" (2021)
Yau Tong, Kowloon

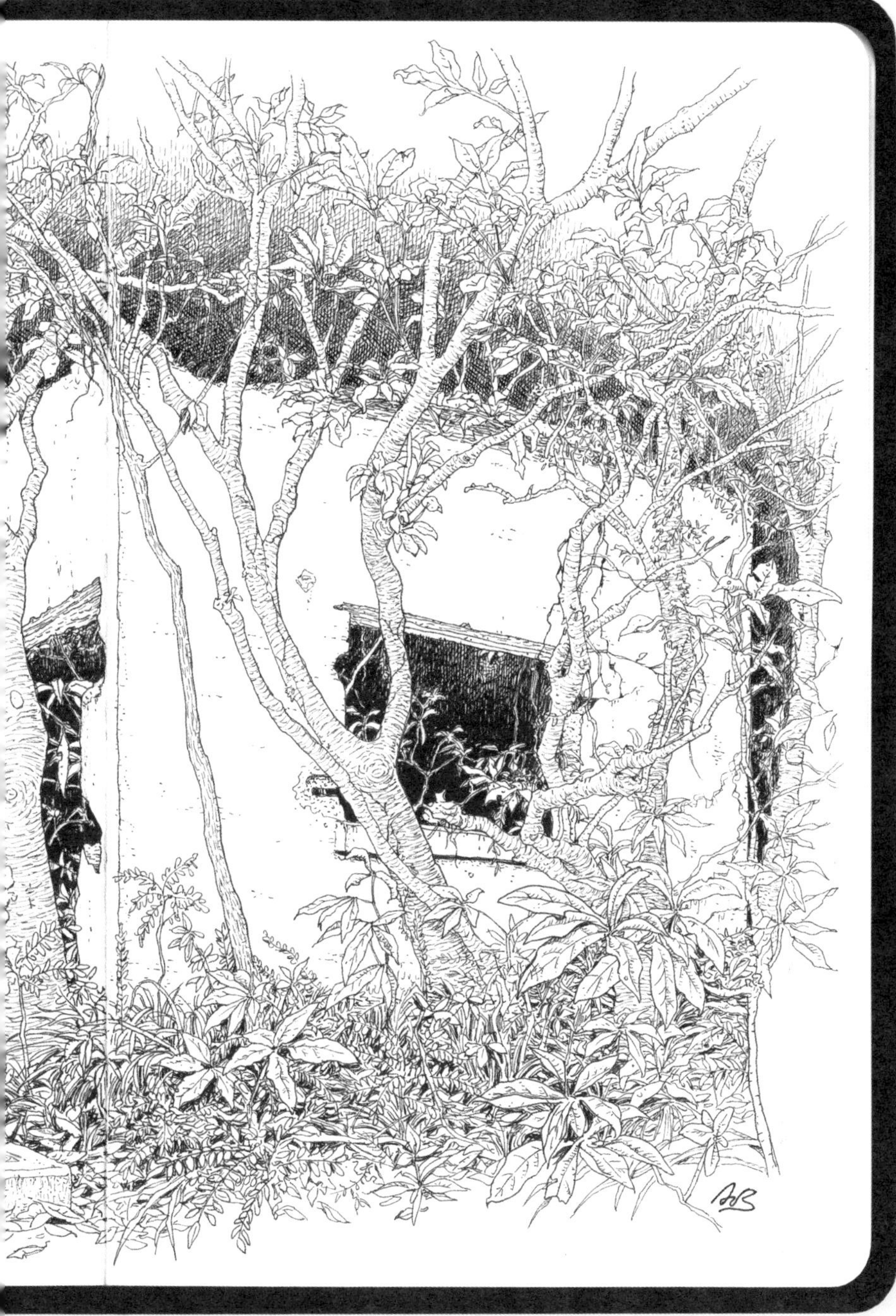

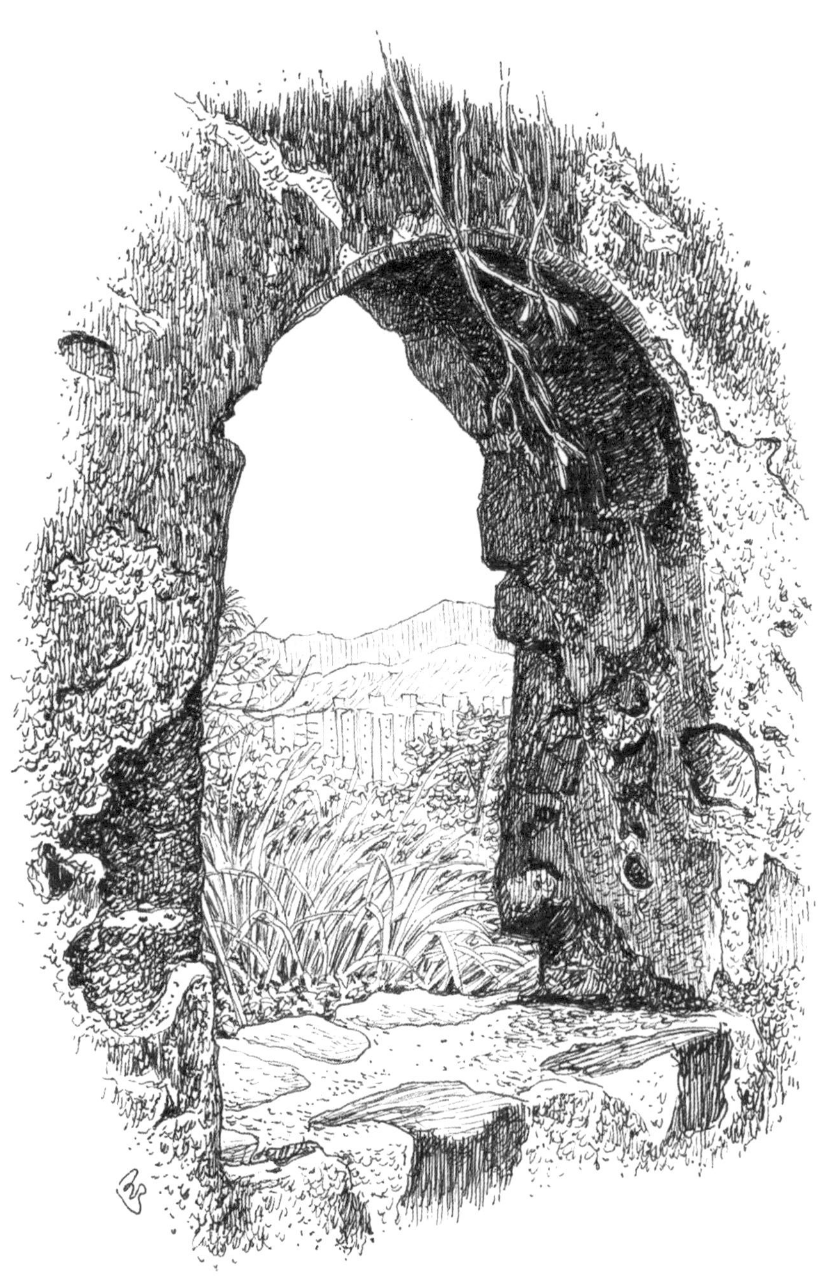

"Observation Post (Window)" (2021)
Mau Wu Shan, Hong Kong

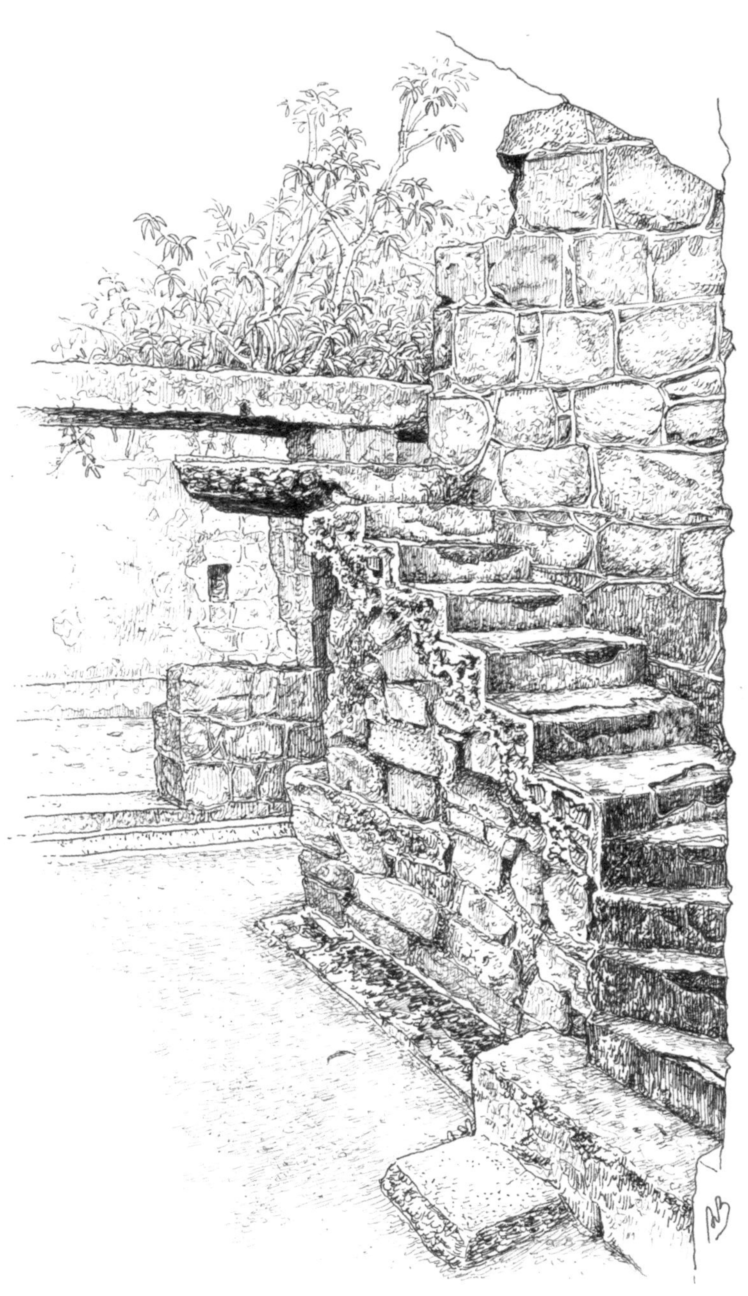

"Observation Post (Stairs)" (2021)
Mau Wu Shan, Hong Kong

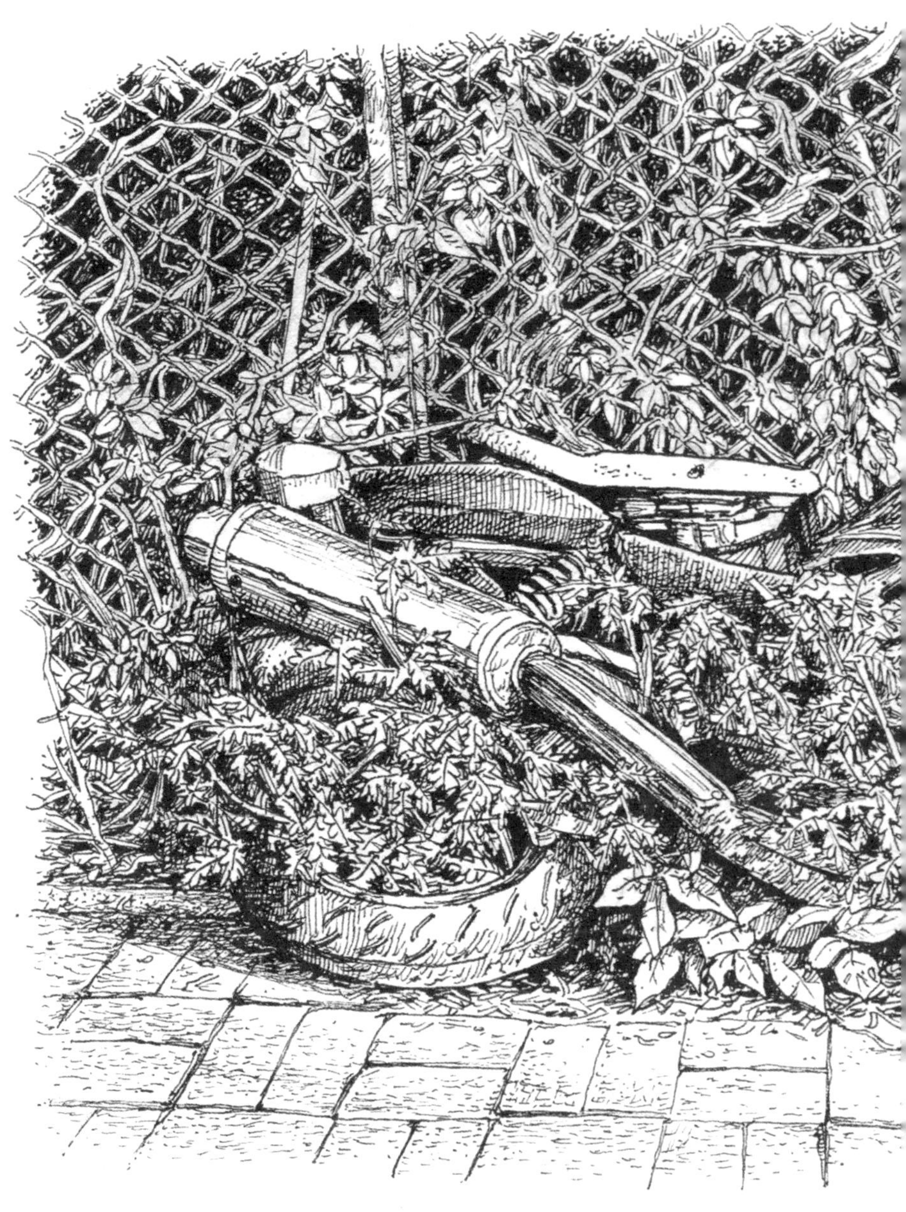

"Time Devours All Things" (2021)
Lohas Park, Hong Kong

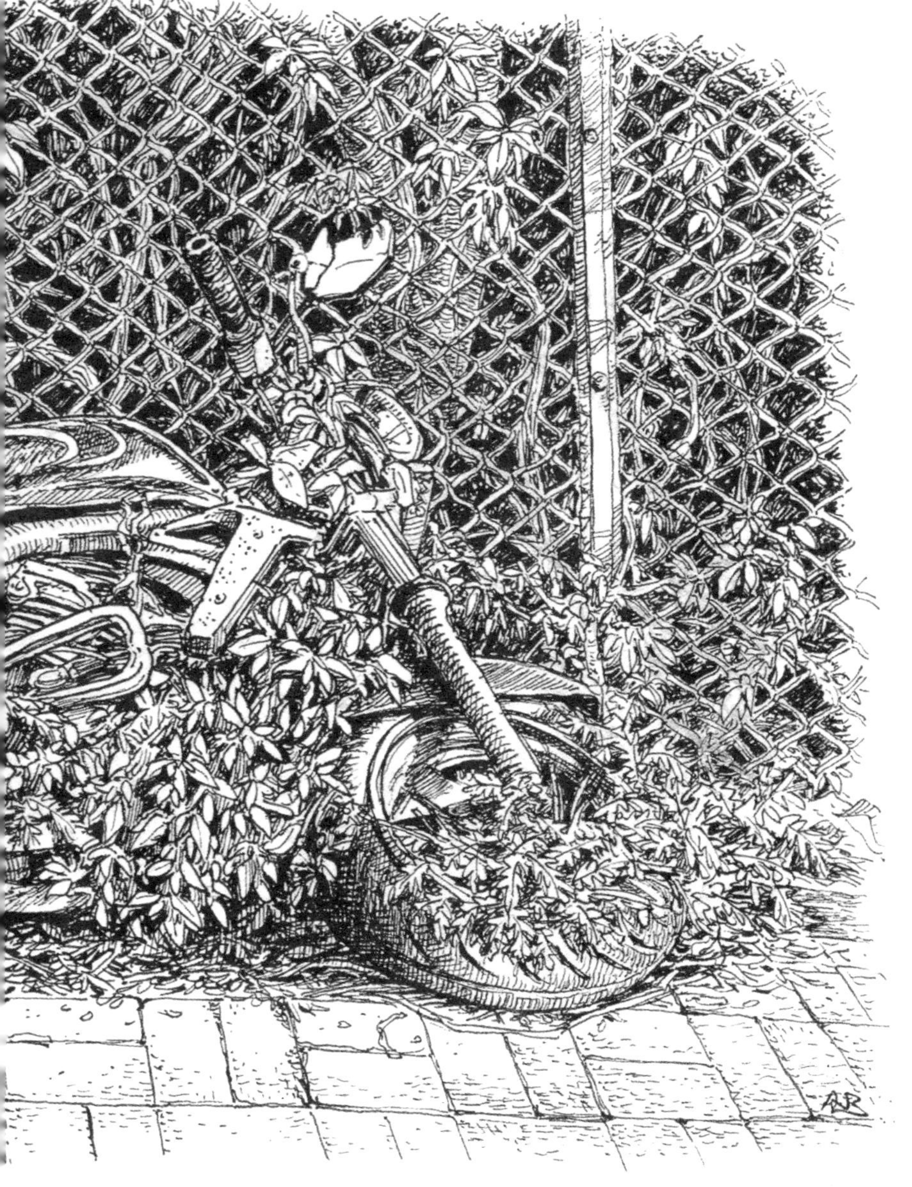

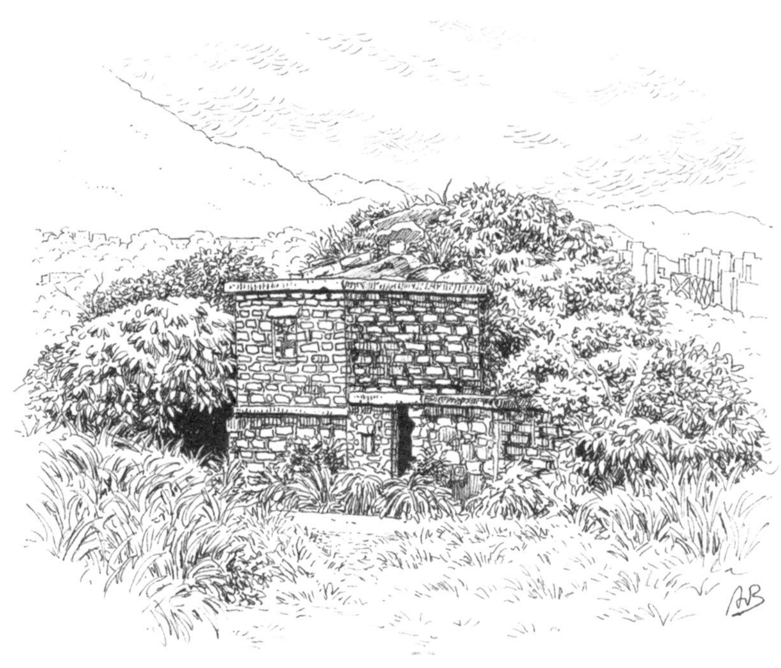

The old stone quarry of Lei Yue Mun is situated only a short (and by "short" I mean 10-15 minutes) walk from the Yau Tong MTR station. I had lived in Hong Kong for about six years before I even learned about it, and this despite how close it was to my home.

After doing a bit of research, I found that the quarry had been active from the early 19th century, all the way up until the late 1980s, when demand finally went on the decline. Thus, it had since been abandoned and to this day, several of its stone structures still stand (well, parts of them, at least).

Behind the ruins, a steep stone wall towers high above. It's an impressive sight. I should add, however, that my feelings of awe were quickly exchanged for adrenaline near the end of my first visit, when two barking dogs came running straight towards me, seemingly out of nowhere. I had the tip of my umbrella pointed toward them (a man near me on the path had also frozen in his tracks) when, for whatever reason, they stopped and ran back the way they came.

Right: ***"Quarry Ruins"*** (2021)
Lei Yue Mun, Hong Kong

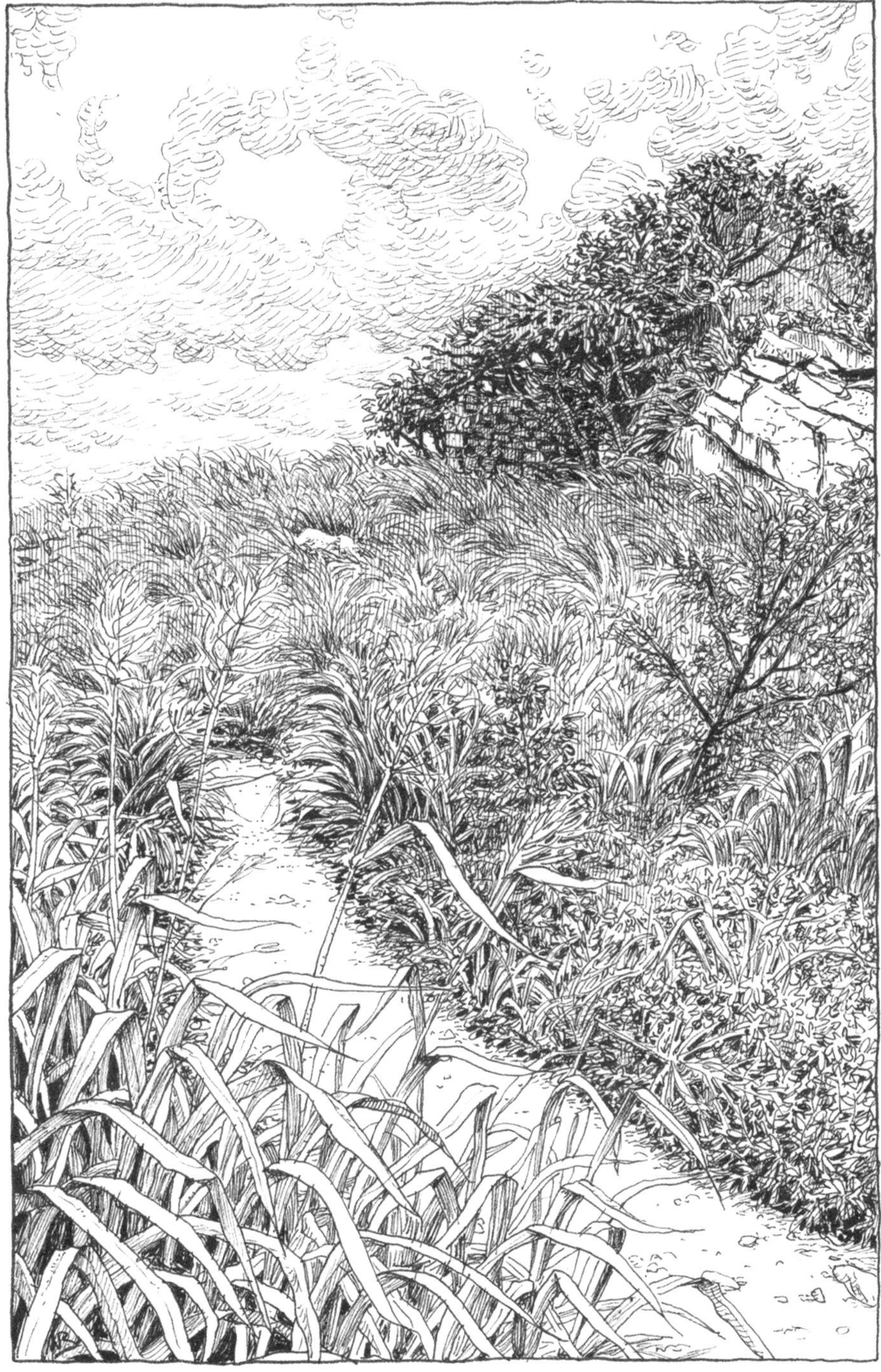

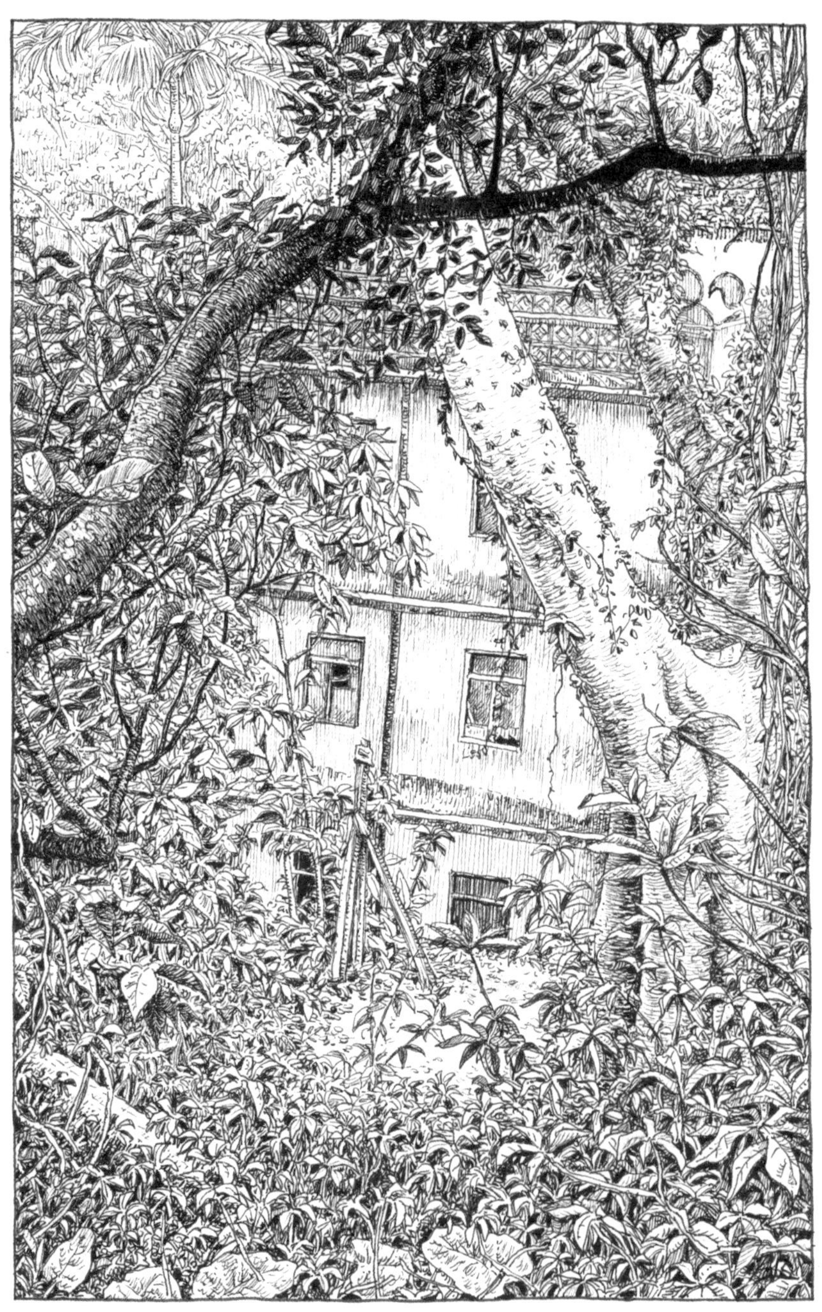

"Ma Wan Ruins" (2022)
Ma Wan, Hong Kong

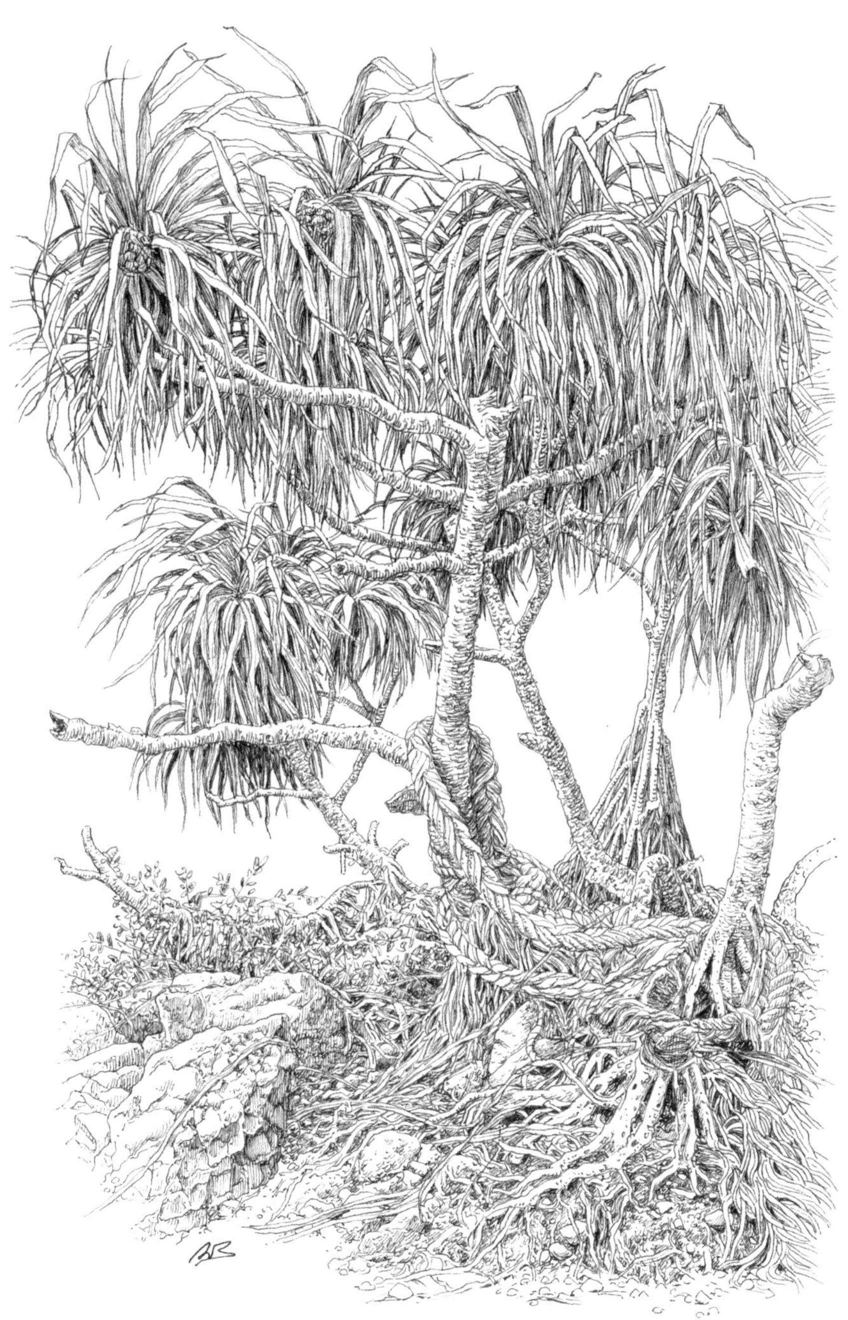

"Tied Up" (2023)
Kat O ("Crooked Island"), Hong Kong

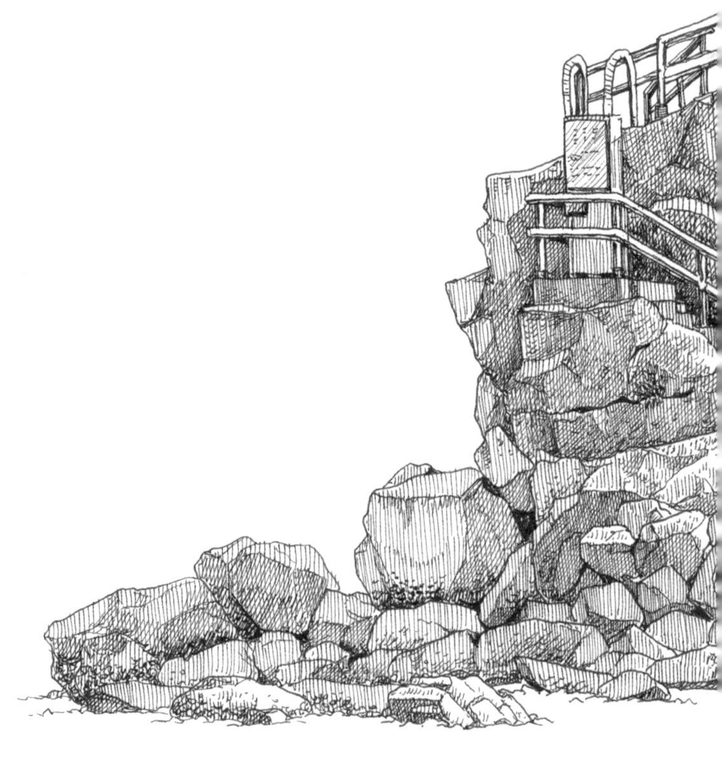

"Beacon" (2020)
Yau Tong, Hong Kong

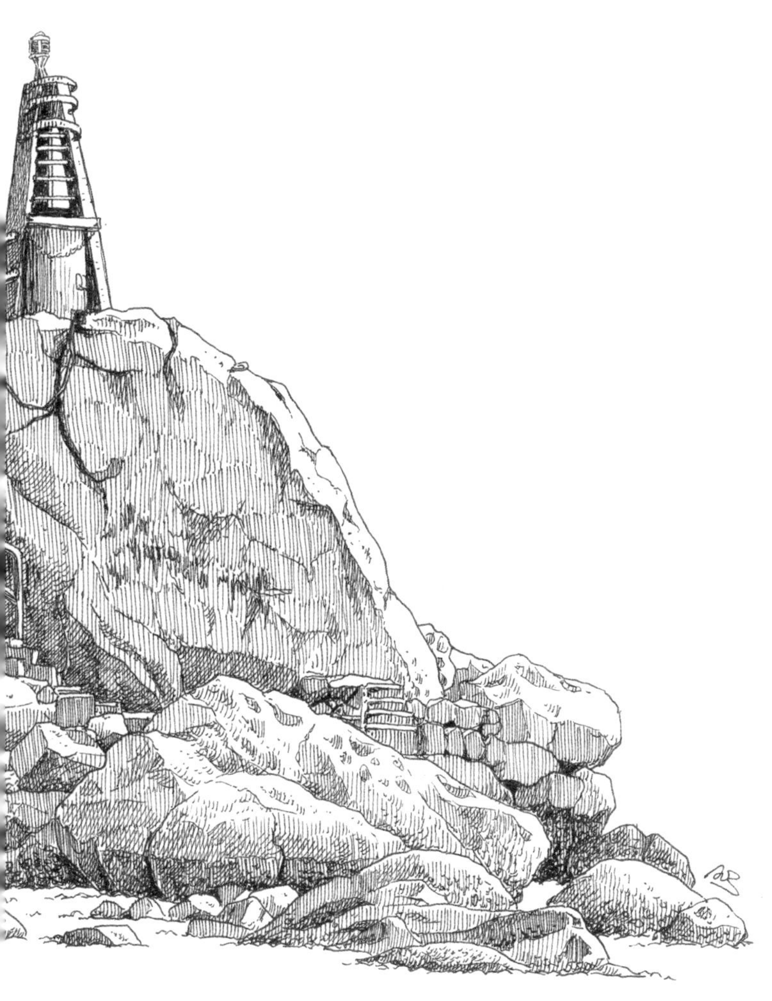

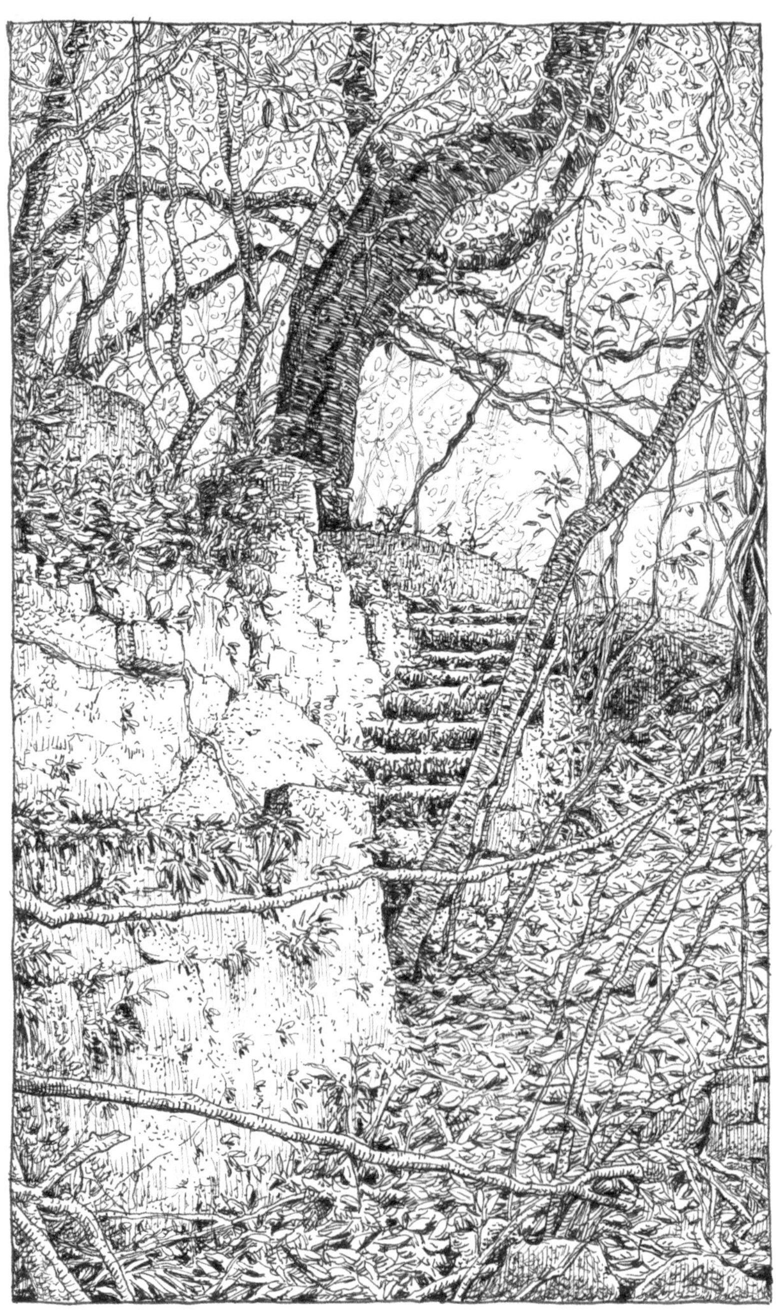

"Ahead On Our Way" (2020)
Braemar Hill, Hong Kong

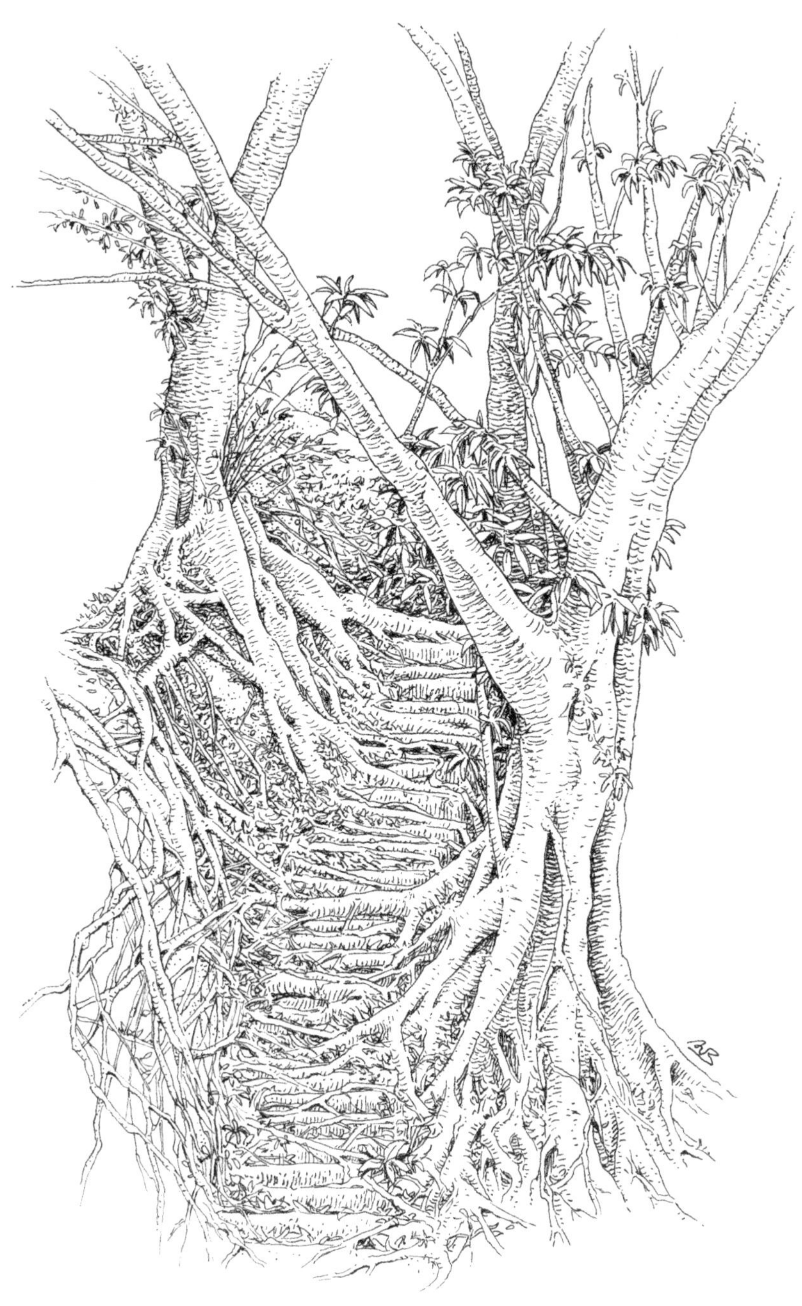

"Stairs" (2020)
Braemar Hill, Hong Kong

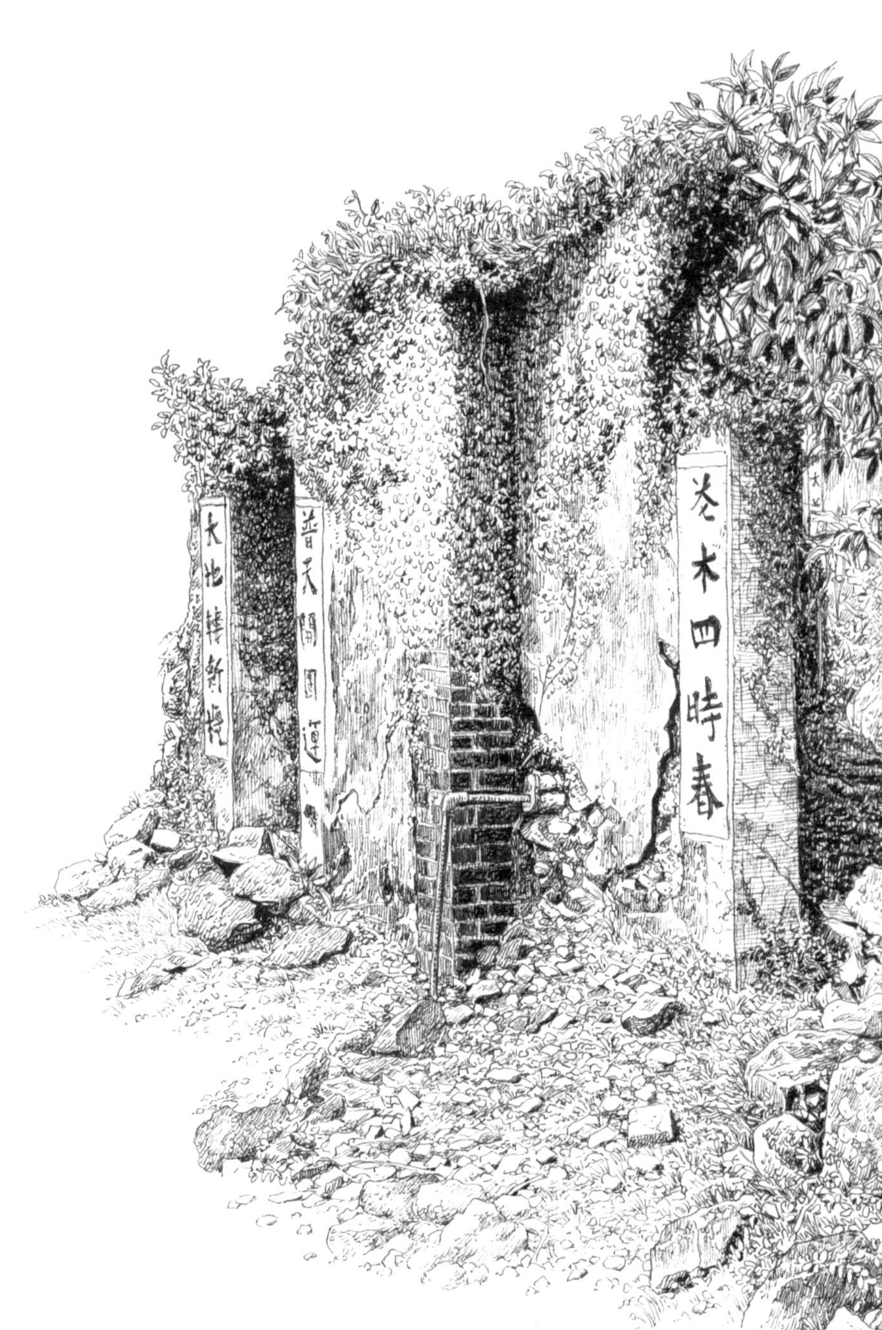
大地轉新機
普天開國運
木四時春

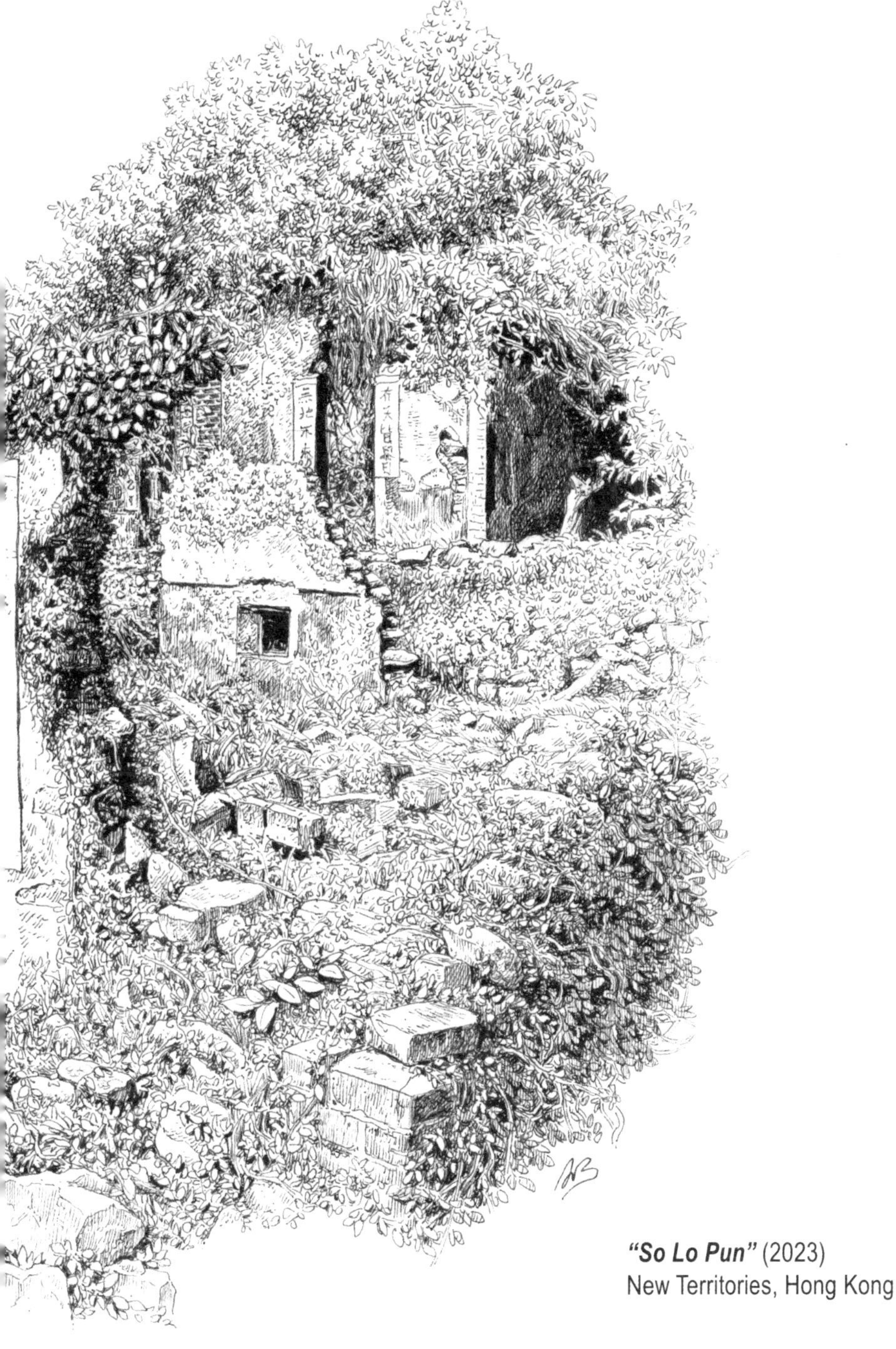

"So Lo Pun" (2023)
New Territories, Hong Kong

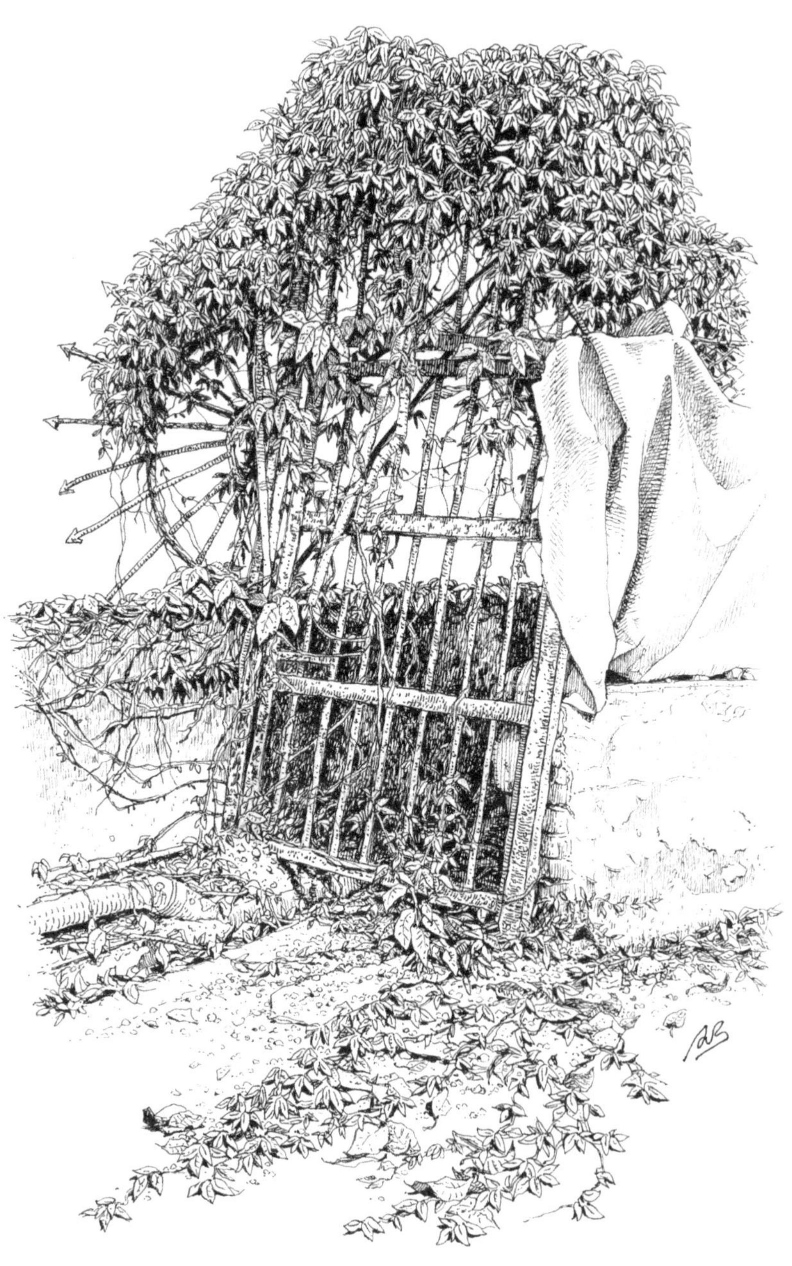

"Rusted Gate" (2022)
North Point, Hong Kong

"Tempus Edax Rerum"

"Time Devours All Things"

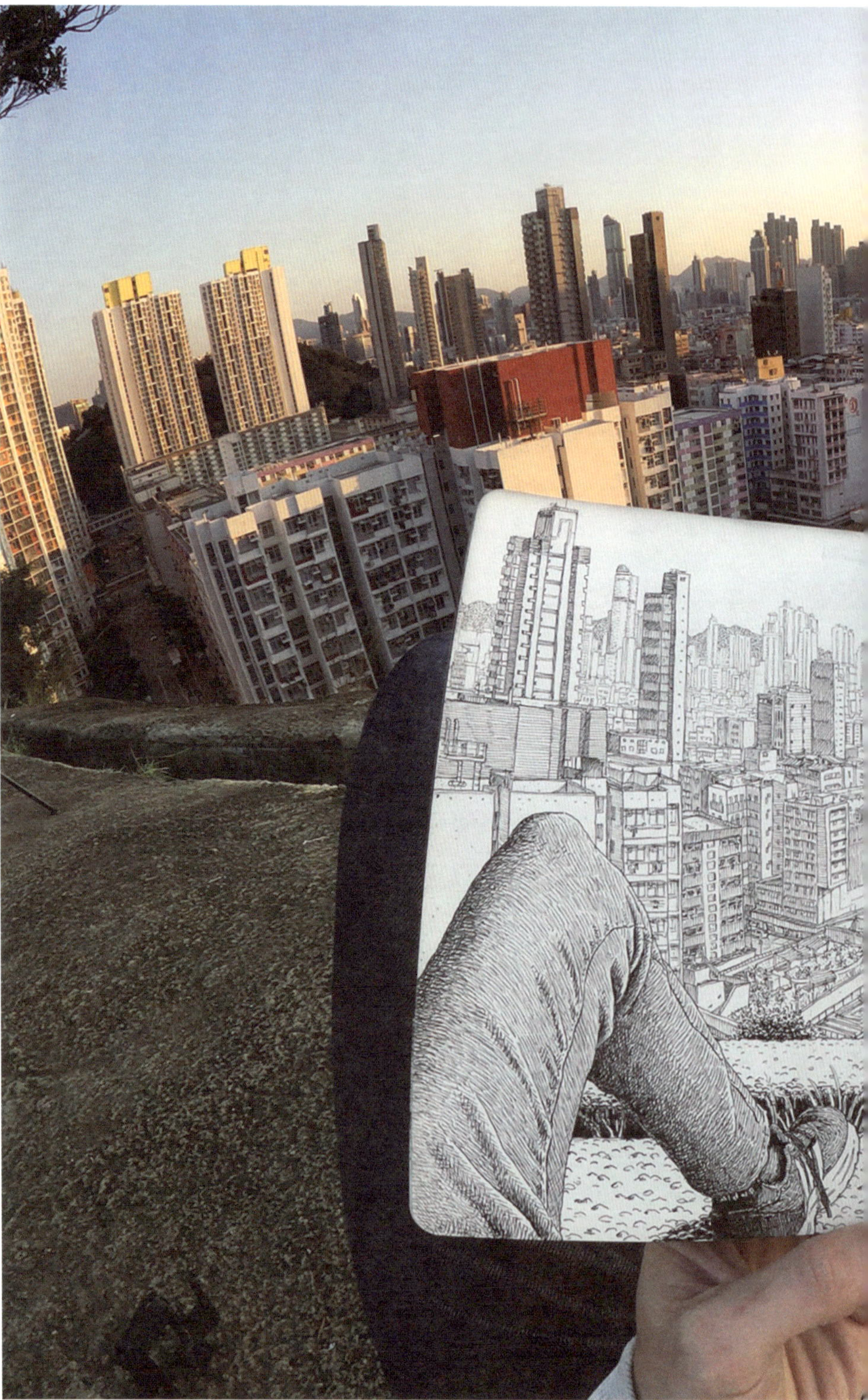

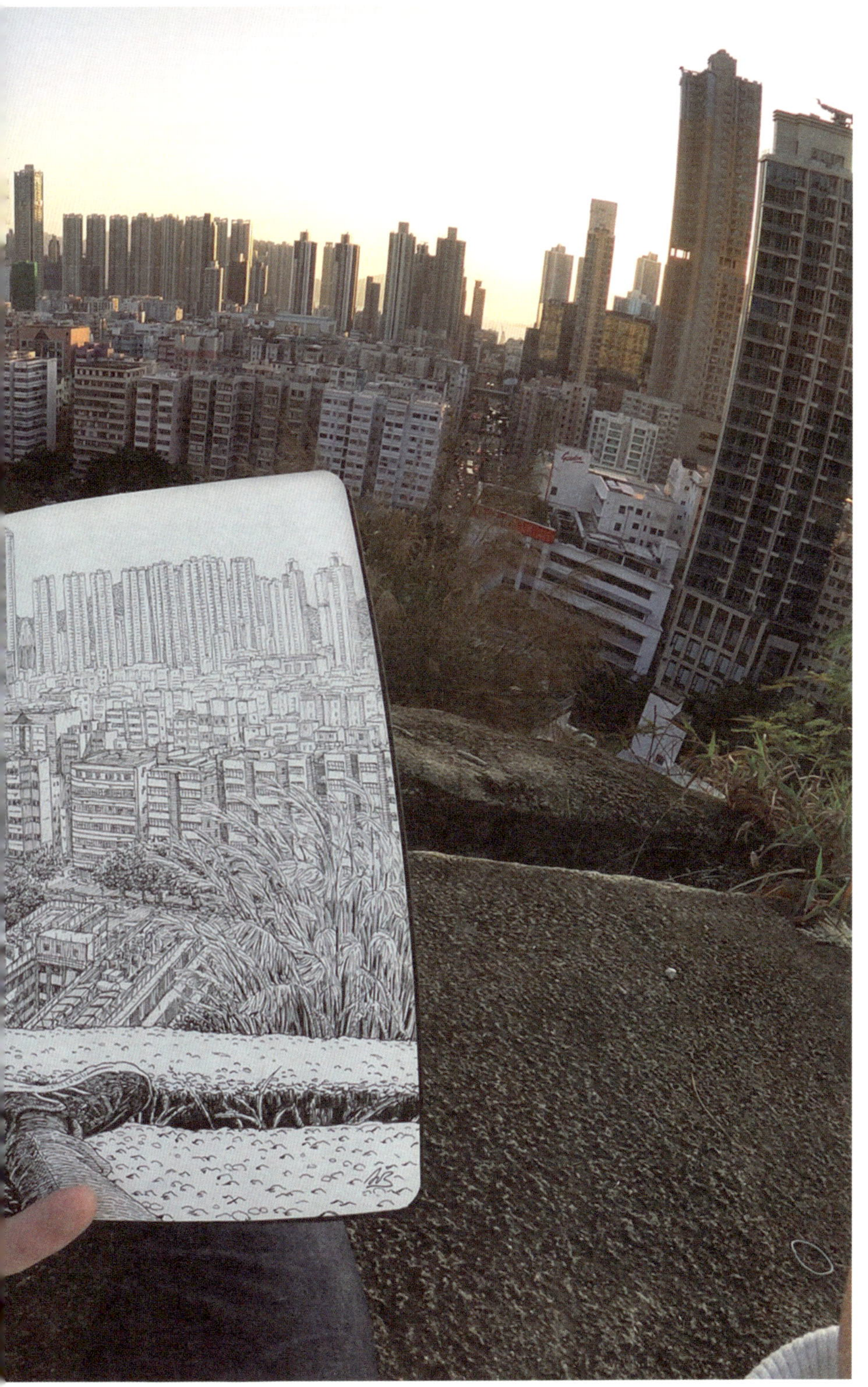

ABOUT THE "ART-OR"

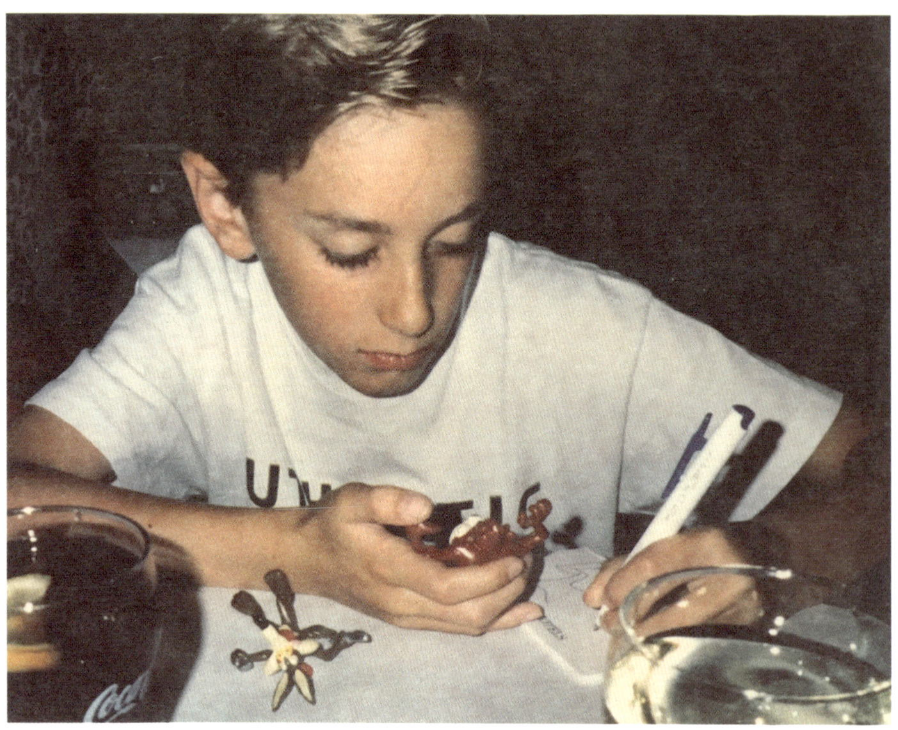

Born and raised in Stockholm, Sweden, Andreas von Buddenbrock has been drawing for as long as he can remember. After graduating from BASIS School of Art in Stockholm in 2011, he went on to pursue a Bachelor of Fine Arts degree in Illustration at the Savannah College of Art and Design in Hong Kong and the U.S. (Savannah and Atlanta, GA).

Following his graduation in 2015, Andreas worked as an assistant to Swedish sculptor Anders Krisár in Manhattan, New York, before training as a Gallery Associate at the Museum of Modern Art.

Today, he spends his time working as an artist and freelance illustrator in Hong Kong under the pseudonym “The Ink Trail”, creating images for both private and commercial clients such as FC Barcelona, Hang Seng Bank, AIA Group, Black Sheep and more. He is the main illustrator of the "World's Largest Coloring Book", which was created in partnership with UBS (Guinness World Record winner 2018).

Working with a collection of fine-liner ink pens, Andreas aims to capture the ambience of the sites he depicts and the personalities of the people he portrays. His love for black and white imagery over the years has pushed him to constantly evolve his realistic drawing style, focusing even more on contrasts, textures and overall composition.

If not found working from his home, he can most likely be seen somewhere outside in nature, sketchbook and pen ready-at-hand.

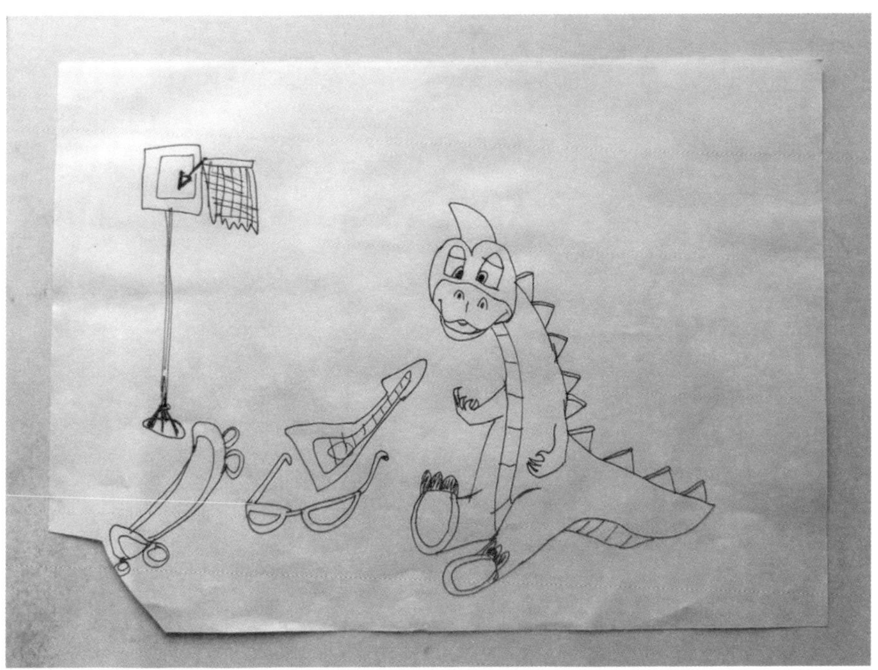

THE PROCESS

So how did these drawings come to be? Like with any creative endeavor, each drawing is the result of a process — one that involves more than a couple of steps.

First, there's the initial inspiration. This can come from places I already know but have been meaning to draw, googling sites around Hong Kong for new ideas of places to visit, or just walking by a spot that's simply too good not to make it into my sketchbook ("I *have* to draw this!").

Second, provided that I'm not already on-site, there's the process of making my way there. This is a point that will naturally vary in terms of difficulty. Sometimes, the spot is behind the building where I live, or inside an air-conditioned museum - simple. Other times, however, the subject in question is located on a steep mountain or in the middle of some forest that's riddled with mosquitoes (not to brag, but these bugs really do love me).

Third, there's the artistic process itself (see images on the right): the initial and more rough pencil outline, the tracing of said outlines with fine-liner ink pens, the addition of details through shading and brushing up of contrasts (a zebra ink pen is great for darkening some shadows and filling in larger black areas) and the final touches to make the drawing look just a little bit more visually appealing. If there is text to be added, this is usually done in a similar fashion, more often than not with the help of my trusted ruler (I don't have the best handwriting when it comes to freehand, so this really helps to keep things in order).

Finally, once the sketch is complete, I'll have it scanned. Dirt, dust and unwanted specks of ink tend to get cleaned away in Photoshop, though sometimes I will leave some of them in order to retain the drawing's authenticity.

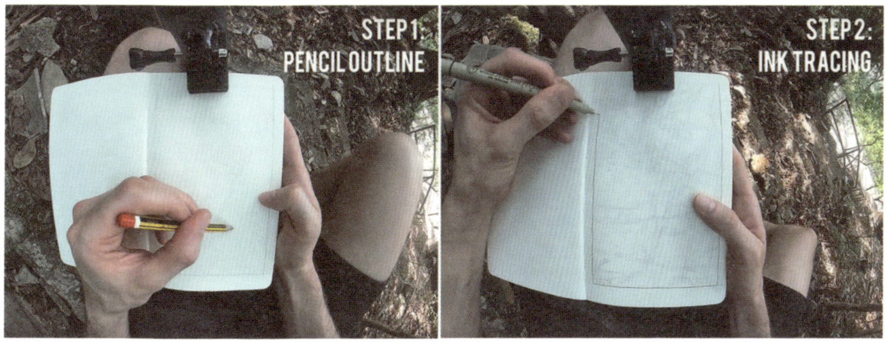

OK, so that covers the creative process. But I know there's a burning question still in your mind, one that I've been asked countless times: "Do you make these sketches there on the spot, or do you take a photo and work off of that?" The answer, when it comes to the sketches in this book ("Monster" not included), is both "yes" and "no". First off, I've made it a rule to always begin these drawings on-site. They take somewhere between five and 10 hours to make and to be safe I will usually snap a photo at some point during the process. For example, I may need to leave suddenly or there's a chance my subject will not be there the next time I come back. This photo is then used as a reliable reference.

The amount of time spent on-site versus off-site will then vary from drawing to drawing. For a majority of the sketches in this book, I'd say that process has been about 80% on-site, while 20% was spent working off of my photo reference. For a few of the more intricate drawings, however, like "Victoria Peak", "Sham Shui Po", "New Horizons", "Kowloon Peak" and "Infinity", this process was done more or less fully on-site. That meant that I would have to come back to the same spot a number of times before the drawing could be completed.

Mosquito bites, sweaty clothes and cold winds: all ignored for the sake of the arts!

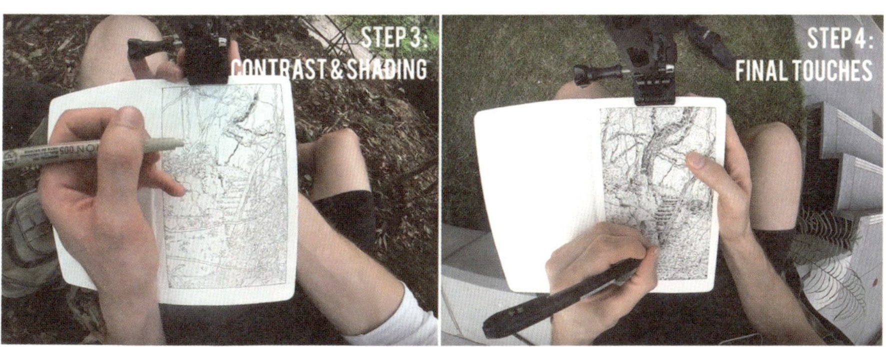

EXHIBITIONS

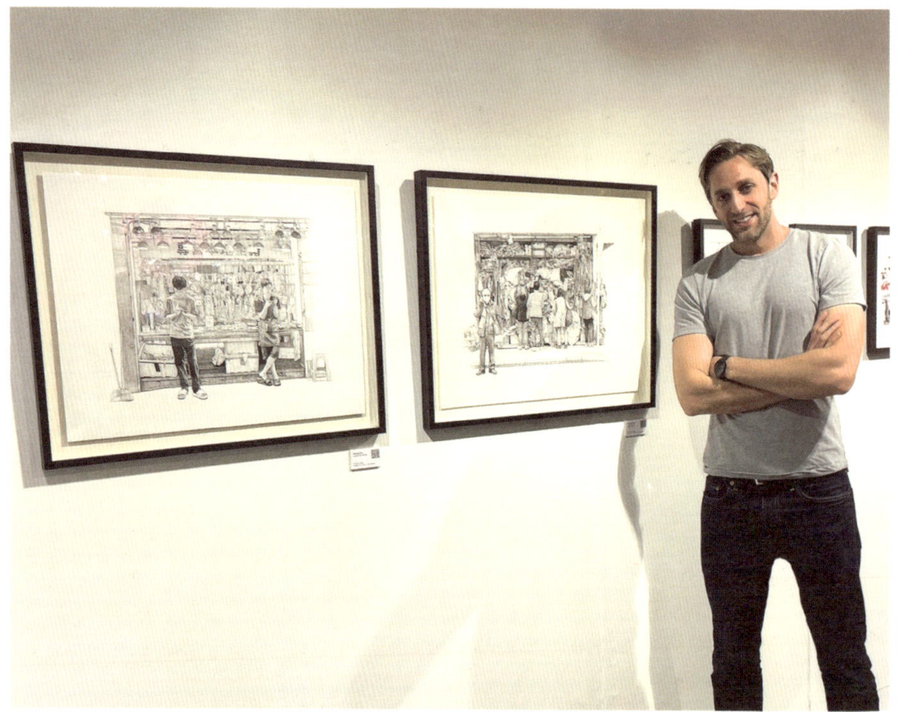

"Pockets", Hong Kong Arts Collective, Wan Chai, Hong Kong, Oct 2023 Photo: Kyra Campbell

Though there is great joy in being inspired and creating new drawings, a lot of the fulfillment also comes from sharing it with other people. I've been very fortunate over these past few years, having had numerous opportunities to showcase my work, whether in publications, solo shows or at fairs and group exhibitions alongside great artistic talents. Shows don't only provide a chance to share with people what I've been working on, but also allow time to meet friends (old and new) and make plans for future projects. Additionally, it's a way to share my creative process with the people I talk to and (I hope) inspire other upcoming artists.

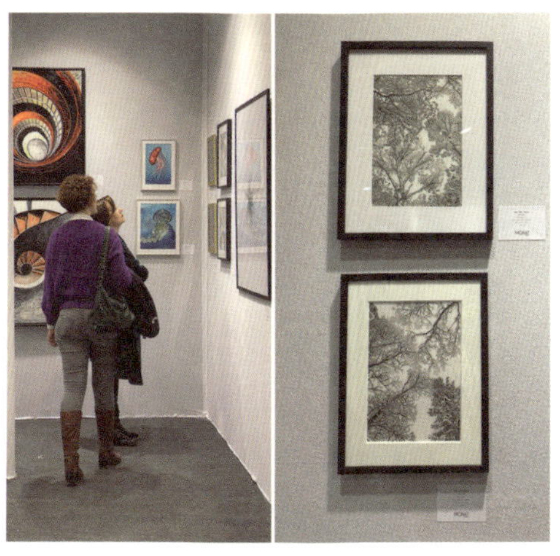

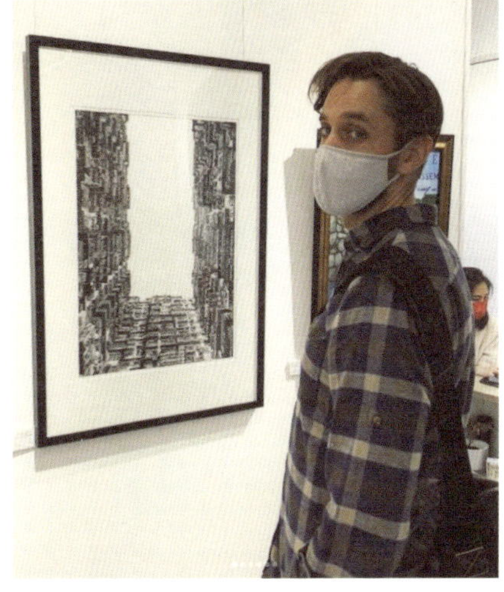

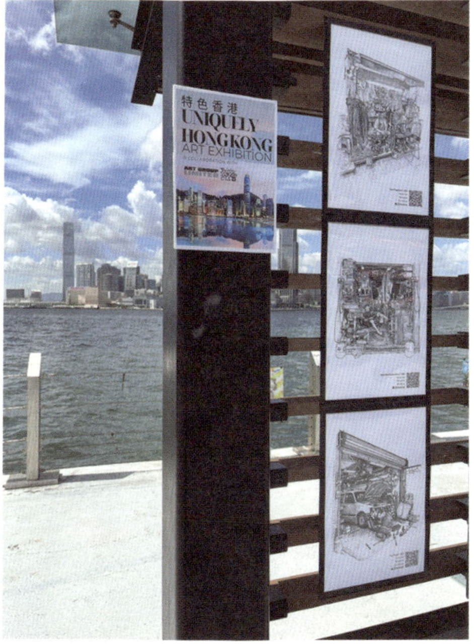
特色香港
UNIQUELY
HONGKONG
ART EXHIBITION
ART GROUP

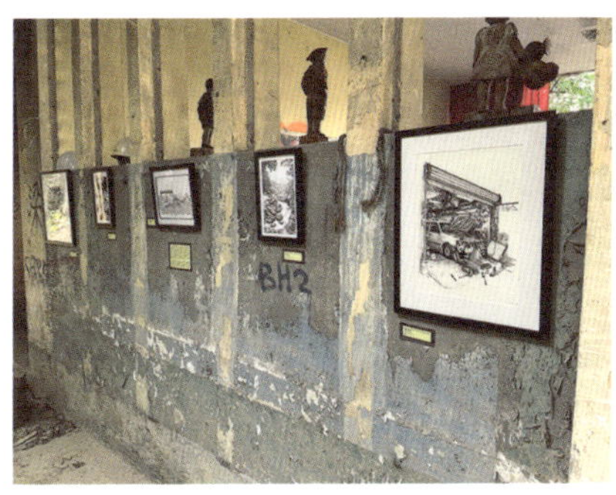
BH2

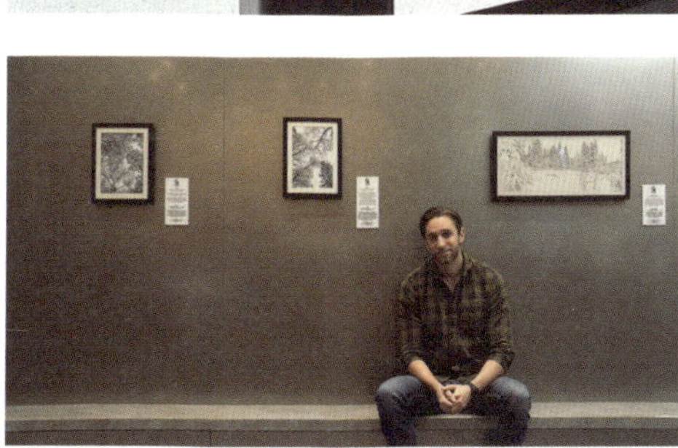

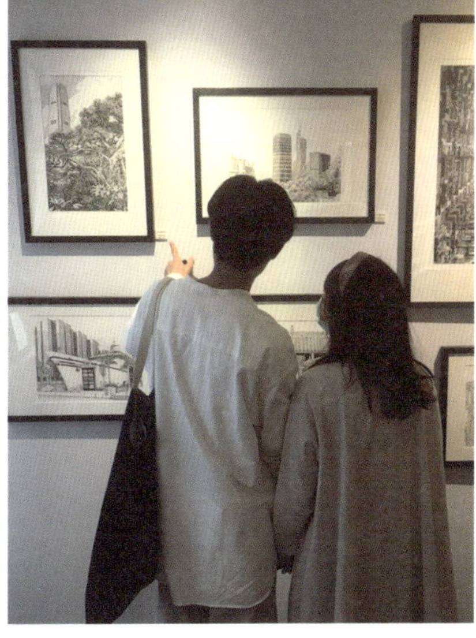

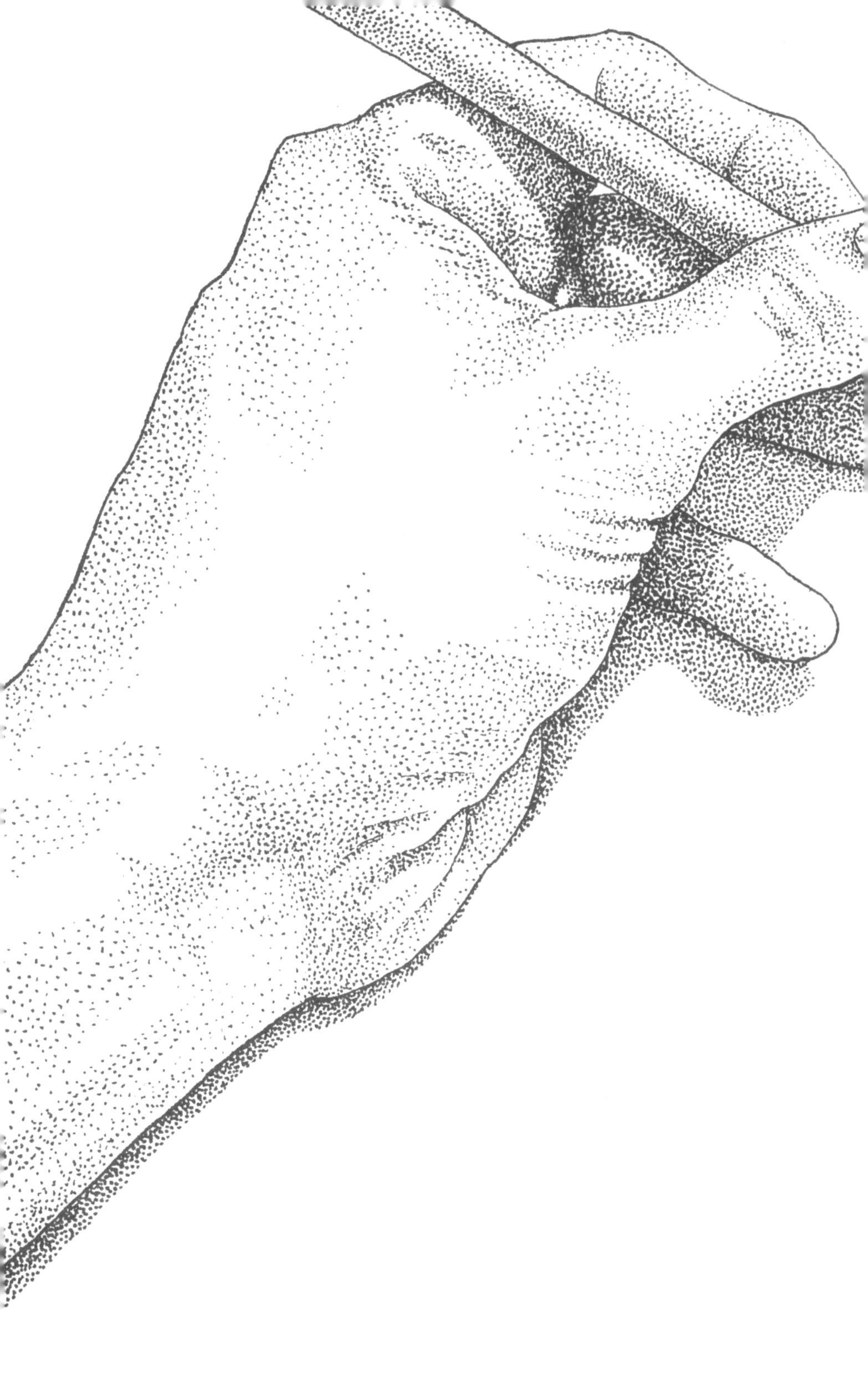

THANK YOU!

Thanks to everyone who has supported, inspired and motivated me over the years. This is to my family who have always had my back, and to my friends and social media following who have made sure to show up at any given exhibition with nothing but kind words and encouragement. You all made this book happen. And, of course, thank *You* for picking up this book! I sincerely hope you enjoyed it.

See you on the trail!

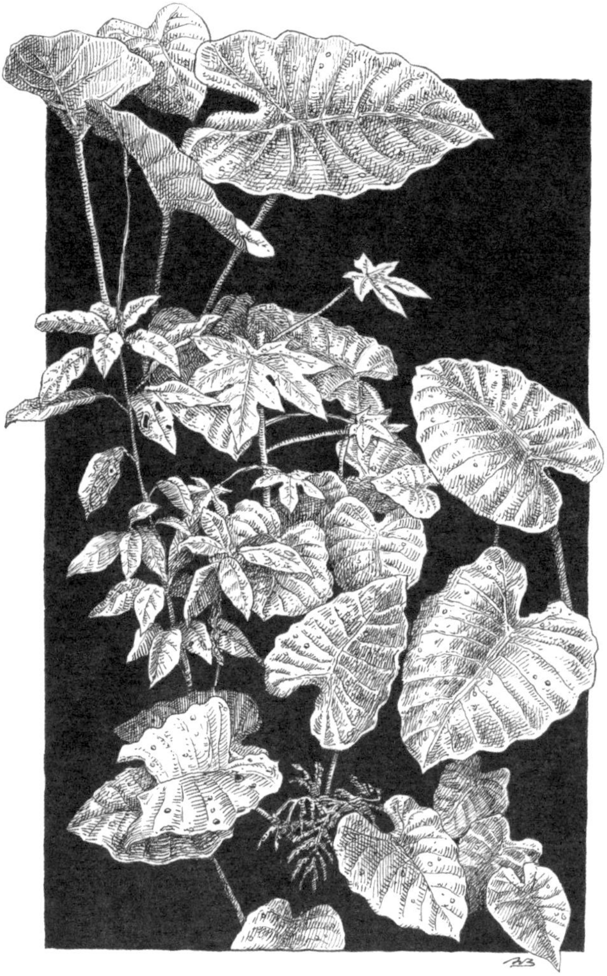

theinktrail

TheInkTrail.com